I0819430

Healthy with a Side of Happy

Healthy WITH A SIDE OF Happy

100 Plant-Based Recipes to Feed Your Family

SABRINA RUDIN

Photographs by Linda Pugliese

NEW YORK

Union Square & Co.
Hachette Book Group
1290 Avenue of the Americas, New York, NY 10104
unionsquareandco.com
@unionsqandco

First Edition: April 2026

Union Square & Co. is an imprint of Grand Central Publishing, a division of Hachette Book Group, Inc. The Union Square & Co. name and logo are registered trademarks of Hachette Book Group, Inc.

Editors: Amanda Englander and Caitlin Leffel
Designer: Renée Bollier
Photographer: Linda Pugliese
Food Stylist: Monica Pierini
Prop Stylist: Paige Hicks
Project Editors: Ivy McFadden and Donna Wright
Production Manager: Kevin Iwano
Copy Editor: Mark McCauslin

Library of Congress Cataloging-in-Publication Data has been applied for.
ISBNs: 978-1-4549-5658-7 (hardcover); 978-1-4549-5659-4 (ebook)

Printed in China

APS

10 9 8 7 6 5 4 3 2 1

"Let food be thy medicine."
-HIPPOCRATES

FOR MY MOM, who knew that food is medicine, and who had the courage to write her own recipe, in the kitchen and in life.

AND FOR LUKAS, DYLAN, AND OLIVER, my most divine and delicious creations. This book, and everything I cook, is for you.

Contents

Introduction

MY MOM ALWAYS SAID, "YOU ARE WHAT YOU EAT."

The seeds for this book were planted when I was a child. Luckily for me, my parents were early disciples of the healthy-foods movement and raised me mostly vegetarian on organic and whole foods. Think carrot juice, kale salad, and tofu, before any of that was mainstream. My most vivid memories of my mom are of her in our family kitchen, washing, chopping, and transforming whole ingredients like candy-striped beets, chickpeas, and pearls of quinoa into nourishing dishes. She didn't consider cooking a chore; she took great pride in making the most beautiful and delicious meals and stocking our refrigerator and pantry with healthy foods. Her passion for cooking for the people she loved was contagious and is one of the biggest reasons I found my way into a natural and organic lifestyle.

Some of you may know me from my restaurants, Spring Café Aspen, but for those of you who don't, let me give you a little introduction into who I am and why I wrote this book. I'm a girl who loves her kitchen. Grocery shopping is my favorite activity, and I will travel far and wide for a vegan soft serve or a loaf of gluten-free sourdough. If I'm not working in the Cafés, I'm usually in my kitchen whipping something up for my three young boys, who always seem to be hungry for their next snack or meal and to whom I love to introduce new and exciting foods. I think I've gotten pretty good at preparing healthy food in a way that is delicious and satisfying. I believe that learning to cook is the single best gift you can give yourself and your family, and it has become my mission to gently guide others toward a less processed and more wholesome way of cooking and eating.

I often think back to my childhood kitchen, the countertop laden with trays of sunflower and broccoli seeds sprouting under the light; the warm stovetop always adorned with a pot of soup or stew bubbling away; and the delicious scent of freshly baked blueberry-carob chip muffins wafting upstairs to my bedroom on cold winter mornings. I didn't know it then, but these experiences would eventually lead me to care deeply about what I put into my body later in life. My mom was a devotee of Hippocrates, whose core philosophy was that food is medicine. Food has the power to heal us or to make us sick. What we eat profoundly impacts our emotional, physical, and spiritual state. Most people don't understand the correlation between what they consume and how they feel, but food is central to our well-being. With a little knowledge and practice, we can avoid highly processed foods and ingredients and start thoroughly enjoying whole, healthy foods. Changing the way you eat will most certainly change your life.

I try to create the same experience of wholesome nourishment in my own home that my mom did for me. My hope is that with this book, and the recipes and methods I'm sharing, the seeds of cooking healthfully might begin to sprout for all of you too.

What Healthy Eating Means These Days and the Kind of Food You'll Find in This Book

When people ask me what I eat, my first answer is always, "Everything," and then I elaborate by saying, "I eat whole, unprocessed, delicious, mostly plant-based food!" You'd think people would get the picture, but it inevitably brings about more questions. In our diet-obsessed, healthy-but-not culture, a natural, organic, and mostly plant-based diet is hard to explain, let alone to navigate. These days, conversations about food start with what to leave *out* and what *not to do*, and that has never resonated with me. This is a book about what gets left *in*, and what *to do* with all the wonderfully delicious fruits and vegetables, beans and grains, and naturally sweet and savory foods available to us: how to choose them, how to prep them, how to cook them, and ultimately, how to thrive on them. My goal is to help you eliminate many processed foods from your diet and learn to rely on whole, organic ingredients instead, without losing any of the deliciousness!

The only thing you won't see in these pages is fish or meat, and that is because, while I don't believe that a fully plant-based diet is right for everyone, I do deeply and wholeheartedly know that eating more fruits, vegetables, and whole foods is essential to our health and vitality, and to that of our planet's. Many of us still don't know how to properly shop for, prepare, and cook delicious and satisfying vegetarian food. The recipes here are from my childhood kitchen, my own kitchen, and the kitchens at my restaurants, Spring Café Aspen. They are elegant but simple and not intimidating to prepare. You will be amazed at how easily you can whip up a delicious and nutritious meal, whether that meal is dinner for one, a family of five, or a group of friends gathered around a table. I'm going to teach you how to cook healthy food that tastes great and that is easy and efficient to prepare. The recipes work to fit any meal or occasion and can be adapted to satisfy the palate of the tiniest eater just starting solids or the appetite of the most mature and hungriest person at the table.

The purpose of this book is to show you how to lay the foundation for healthy cooking and eating in your own life, and how to build on your new skills to feed yourself and your family. Once you master that, you'll be amazed at how confident you feel and how much joy being in the kitchen can bring. Taking ownership of your food and your health is so empowering. If you follow the recipes and methods that I've laid out for you, you will learn how to eat a healthier, more organic, nourishing diet, prepare satisfying meals, and detox your kitchen from the top offenders. I hope you use this knowledge to shop, cook, and eat beautiful and delicious food. Let's get started, because feeling good about what you're cooking and eating is within reach.

LET'S TALK ABOUT THE BASICS

I have four basic principles for cooking healthy meals and enjoying nutritious food

- **STICK TO ORGANIC WHOLE FOODS WHENEVER POSSIBLE:** These are foods we should all be eating more of, foods that set us up for health and vitality and steer us away from inflammation and chronic disease. Buy organic whenever possible, especially when consuming foods on the Environmental Working Group's Dirty Dozen list (which is the list of the most heavily sprayed fruits and vegetables). Avoid heavily processed foods and look for real ingredients; if you don't know how to pronounce a certain ingredient, you probably don't want to be consuming it.

- **EMBRACE THE RITUAL OF MEALTIME, AT LEAST TWICE A WEEK**: Whether you invite a few friends over for dinner or sit down to eat with your family, celebrate the ritual of cooking, setting a table, and enjoying a meal. There are many days that I'm guilty of standing over the counter and racing through lunch while finishing emails. Being more mindful about *how* you eat is the first step toward changing *what* you eat, and this becomes even more important as you start a family. I believe deeply that the more we model healthy behaviors and relationships with food for our kids, the better chance we have that they will make good and healthy choices as they grow up. The meals my kids eat the most at are ones when we all sit down together, the food is served family style, and they can help themselves to whatever they think looks good. If you have a child who is just starting solids, sit and eat with them, let them watch what you are consuming, and allow them to experiment with picking from your bowl or asking for a bite. Eating is a learned behavior. The best memories are made around a table.

- **SWAP OUT THE JUNK AND FEEL GOOD ABOUT INDULGING:** Create a pantry and a refrigerator where nothing is off limits or forbidden and where you can feel good about reaching for whatever you are craving. I have a big sweet tooth, and dessert is an important part of my life, but processed ingredients and refined sugars don't have to be. Choose natural sweeteners like date sugar and pure maple syrup when you want to have something sweet. I am all about balance, but understanding ingredients and doing my research allows me to keep the main offenders, like food dye and toxic preservatives, out of our pantry so that everyone in my home can feel good about indulging a sweet tooth or reaching for a snack.

- **WHEN YOU CAN, SWITCH TO HOMEMADE:** The easiest way to eat healthy food is to make it yourself. Homemade versions of your favorite things are often tastier, more affordable, and a lot cleaner than their store-bought counterparts. Packaged food should ideally be made of only three or four ingredients, but most of these products have gums, fillers, and processed ingredients to make them last longer. Take stock of your fridge and pantry and see what store-bought products you use that you can start making yourself. You'd be amazed that most everyday staples are simple to make at home. In our family, for example, we prepare our own salad dessing, granola, and hummus. What are some things you and your family love to eat daily? Maybe it's a morning smoothie, plant-based milk for your coffee, or your child's favorite applesauce. With a few tips and tricks that I'll teach you, you can make these favorites at home and feel great about what's in them.

FEEDING OURSELVES, FEEDING OUR FAMILIES

I spend most of my time thinking about food: what to cook, what to eat, and what to feed my family. We live in a world of fad diets and ever-changing health advice, and it's hard to keep track. When you're trying to cook nutritiously while keeping up with the commitments of everyday life, it can be daunting. As a working mom with three active boys, I know it can feel overwhelming to think about sitting down for a nourishing lunch or taking the time to cook dinner at the end of a long day, but here's the beautiful truth: With the right ingredients, an arsenal of easy-to-follow recipes, and a little practice, cooking food that is healthy and delicious doesn't have to be time-consuming or hard. I have between thirty minutes and one hour each evening to make dinner for my family, and I've had enough conversations with friends and strangers to know that I'm not alone. The good news is that if you put in the small amount of time and effort it takes to learn to cook healthy meals, you'll feel better, get inspired in the kitchen, and have more energy to tackle the rest of your day. Eating wholesome food that tastes great doesn't need to be complicated, so let's demystify it.

When I became a mom for the first time, it was even more important to me to cook the healthiest foods for my family. I was lucky to be able to turn to the recipes and knowledge that my mom passed on to me and build from there. I researched and refamiliarized myself with all the nutrient-dense ingredients I learned about in my childhood, I created a nontoxic kitchen by making small changes that have had a big and lasting impact, and I began experimenting in the kitchen, cooking most nights of the week and making a point to eat meals as a family or invite friends over for dinner to taste-test my new recipes and dishes. Cooking became my touchstone. It brought me comfort, clarity, and satisfaction, both mentally and physically. I was nourished and nurtured, and I felt good about what I was eating and feeding the ones I love.

I hope this book will serve as a road map for anyone who wants to begin to take the steps toward living a healthier and more balanced life. I hope it gets you into the kitchen, takes the pressure off mealtime, and helps you discover a more natural and nutritious way to cook, eat, and live.

TIPS TO COOK HEALTHY FOR A FAMILY

There is nothing more rewarding than preparing a home-cooked meal for your family and enjoying it together around the table. When it comes to cooking for my family, I have one rule: It must be a meal that works for everyone; otherwise, I'm a short-order cook, standing in the kitchen and trying to meet everyone's different whims and requests. The biggest tip I can offer is to try to relax and not pressure your kids to eat when they don't want to, because no one likes to be watched closely and have their bites scrutinized (mamas, I'm looking at all of us here)! Kids eat well when they are relaxed, and if they don't finish their plate every night, that's okay; you can always try again at the next meal. I've spent countless hours experimenting with healthy foods for my kids, and here's what I've come to learn:

- **EAT WITH THEM!** I find that kids respond to three things when it comes to developing a more adventurous palate: bright colors, a delicious dressing or dip, and sharing a meal with a caregiver. People usually ask me how I get my boys to try vegetables and salads, and the answer is always *modeling*. If I want to spark their curiosity, I'll make a big bowl for myself and pull out a few nonthreatening ingredients like olives, cucumber, and red pepper, cut them into very small cubes, toss with a little dressing,

and offer it in a small bowl (with whatever else they are eating) next to mine. Then we sit down together and enjoy. My boys won't always go for it, but usually they dig in and eat alongside me! Don't worry if they refuse. Just keep offering raw veggies at every meal and one day they will surprise you.

- **GO BOLD!** I'm not sure where the myth came from that babies and small children like only plain food, but in my experience, if you start them on flavor early, then flavor is what they will love. Sure, they may go through phases of wanting plain pasta or only simple foods, but these preferences come and go. With a good foundation, our children will always find their way back to healthy eating.

- **INCLUDE THEM IN THE PROCESS!** When invited to the conversation and given a say over their food choices, kids generally respond in a positive way. I include my kids in shopping, prepping, and cooking. We take farmers' market and grocery store trips, and I encourage them to pick out veggies, snacks, and condiments and put them in our carts or baskets. I give them tasks in the kitchen like helping me bake muffins, sautéing onions (under a watchful eye), or peeling fruit and veggies.

- **HAVE HONEST CONVERSATIONS WITH KIDS ABOUT FOOD!** Just as we have age-appropriate conversations about everyday things like kindness and family habits and about bigger topics like social justice and world events, I think we can bring food into the conversation. When my son asks if he can have a snow cone from the park, I'll explain that while it may look pretty, those bright colors don't always make our bodies feel good and there are other fun options at home or from a different shop. Every now and then, I'll say yes to avoid it becoming taboo, but the other times he is more than happy to choose from the health food store and is more likely to finish the healthier treat than the highly processed one. That's the beauty of raising our kids this way. Taste buds are made, not born!

GRAIN FREE
TORTILLA CHIPS
DAIRY FREE
NACHO
GRAIN FREE
TORTILLA CHIPS
Sea Salt
jovial
jovial
Sunfood
nutiva
Simple Mills
Ghia
QUINOA
pasta
pasta
tomatoes
baking
seaweed
herbal tea
baking
cereal

Healthy Pantry, Healthy Life: A Setup for Success

Cooking healthy and vibrant meals begins with having a fridge and pantry well stocked with nutritious food. If you're like me, you're much more likely to cook a beautiful meal if you're not scrambling to find ingredients at the end of a busy day. It's cliché, but when it comes to cooking, preparation is key. While some people find grocery shopping to be an onerous chore, I think of it as one of life's great pleasures. It can feel tedious, especially when it's the final item on a long to-do list, so try to infuse a little adventure into your weekly grocery run. The best way to do this is to explore your local farmers' market, where you can get to know the farmers and growers making your food and discover new varietals that you wouldn't find in the supermarket aisles. If you're going to a local health food store, take a few moments to browse the merchandise, as you would in a clothing store. There are so many healthy and delicious products lining the shelves that might not be on your "list" but will add joy to your grocery haul. Here are some more tips for sourcing, shopping, and organizing your groceries.

BEFORE YOU SHOP

It's easy to get overwhelmed by long shopping lists and hard-to-find specialty items, so all the recipes in this book rely on easy-to-source whole foods (think loads of vibrant veggies), real-food vegetarian protein sources (beans and tofu, anyone?), and my can't-live-without-them seasonings and condiments (hello, tamari). Before I shop, I take a quick scan of my fridge and pantry and make a short list of the things I know I use daily and might be running low on. It's important to have staples, but I also get a lot of inspiration from grocery shopping, and many of my meals are dreamed up while stumbling upon a vibrant purple cauliflower or a local GF sourdough at the greenmarket, or when I find a new and fun condiment, like fermented banana peppers, at the health food store. The takeaway? Always stock the basics, but leave room to get inspired!

FARMERS' MARKETS, SUPERMARKETS, AND HEALTH FOOD STORES: WHERE'S A HOME COOK TO GO?!

I won't lie: I cross New York City in search of the best groceries, but you don't have to. You can find all the items in these recipes at your local supermarket, or you can order them online. If you have some spare time and you're up for an adventure, here's how I think about shopping for groceries and how I break up my list.

- **FARMERS' MARKET:** seasonal vegetables and fruits, local pasture-raised eggs and cheeses, sourdough breads, and specialty items like a pastry from your favorite baker or jars of local hot sauce and honey.
- **HEALTH FOOD STORE:** supplemental produce (like avocados, bananas, and citrus year-round unless you are lucky enough to live in Southern California!), plant-based yogurt and cheeses, and gluten-free dry goods like brown-rice pasta and tortillas.

- **SUPERMARKETS:** Large-scale supermarkets usually have a nice organic section where you can find many basics that you need. Many also have "natural corners" with plant-based cheeses and milks and better-for-you options for your favorite condiments and snacks.
- **ONLINE RETAILERS:** If you're looking for affordable but healthy options for many condiments and dry goods, websites like Thrive Market are a wonderful resource. I also love Glaser Organic Farms for nut butter and for buying nuts, grains, and beans in bulk. I order from Sami's Bakery for gluten-free sandwich bread, rolls, and lavash.

Now that you have an idea of where to shop, here's what I always have in my fridge and pantry.

Fruit

Think of fruit as nature's candy: bright, bountiful, and colorful goodness that is literally sweet as sugar. I try to eat as seasonally and locally as possible. That doesn't mean we don't cut open a pineapple in the winter—we do. But for the most part, I buy what's in season as that is what usually tastes the best and has the lowest environmental impact. Our freezer is always stocked with frozen berries and bananas (using frozen organic fruit is a great way to consume fruits that are out of season, as they are typically harvested at peak ripeness and maintain their nutrients). Rather than buying it at the store in plastic bags, I freeze it myself in silicone containers. My kids drink a lot of smoothies and having frozen fruit on hand is a game changer. I try to always have our fruit bowl laden with citrus, Honeycrisp apples, Asian pears, and assorted melons. Avocados and tomatoes are always on hand in abundance, and, yes, they are technically fruits!

Vegetables

Vegetables are the backbone of our diet and of this book. I deeply believe that the reason many people don't like vegetables is because they don't know the right way to cook them. Eating the same vegetables over and over again can also get monotonous, but there are countless varietals, and I once again encourage you to explore your local farmers' markets and try something new. In the meantime, if you keep these few staples on hand, you'll always be prepared to whip up a quick stir-fry or soup, a morning green smoothie, or a big crunchy salad. If you enjoy a few of these vegetables daily, you'll ensure that your diet is filled with essential plant-based nutrients and minerals. These are the vegetables we tend to eat the most of: Carrots and celery for soups and stews. Mixed greens: bright, crisp romaine, endive, radicchio, and fennel. I use a lot of fennel in juices and salads and just to snack on with a little olive oil and salt. I always have reusable produce bags full of dark leafy greens like kale, bok choy, and napa cabbage; Asian varietals are often more tender, easier to digest, and more user-friendly than better-known dinosaur kale and Swiss chard, so don't be afraid to branch out! Starchy vegetables also appear in many of these recipes; my favorites are sweet potatoes, kabocha squash, delicata squash, and, of course, potatoes. You'll see many a white potato in this book, whether baked, roasted, or mashed—I love a potato, and we eat a lot of them.

Grains and Beans

I lean toward grains that are naturally gluten-free, like rice, quinoa, and buckwheat, as well as gluten-free oats. I like to buy organic grains in bulk, and it's important whenever possible to check if the grains are certified glyphosate-free, a nasty pesticide used in big agriculture that is linked to cancer, infertility, and other health issues. I'm a dried-bean kind of gal; black, pinto, lentils, and chickpeas are my go-tos, and they are featured in many of my recipes. When cooked, ½ cup dried beans will equal 1 (15-ounce) can, or about 1½ cups total. Before using the dried beans, soak them overnight in filtered water to cover, then drain and cook in an Instant Pot or pressure cooker (see page 202) or on the stovetop (see page 198) until tender. I also always keep a few jars or cans of precooked beans in the pantry to easily throw into a soup or stew or to make a quick after-school hummus. I love Jovial brand jarred beans.

Dairy Products

I don't consume or cook with much dairy, as dairy is a highly inflammatory food and no one in my family really tolerates it well. The exceptions are grass-fed butter, organic and pasture-raised local eggs, and raw goat and sheep's-milk cheese. For plant-based options, we love coconut and cashew yogurt; the best brands for mild flavor with the least amount of processed ingredients are Cocojune and Forager Project. I keep Violife vegan mozzarella and Kite Hill cream cheese on hand for pizza nights and bagel mornings.

Nuts and Nut Butters

I rely heavily on nuts and nut butters in my cooking. They add richness without the need to use dairy, are an excellent source of protein, and bring texture and depth to many simple dishes. When buying nuts, I opt for raw, organic, and unsalted. This way I can toast and season them as I like for any recipe. Raw nuts are easier to digest, especially when soaked overnight, as their natural enzymes haven't been destroyed in the heating process. I choose raw nut butters like almond, walnut, and pumpkin seed for extra nutrients in simple recipes like Easy-as-Sliced-Bread French Toast (page 81). My favorite brand for raw and organic nuts and nut butters is Glaser Organic Farms. They take great care in storing, sourcing, and processing their products to prevent them from going rancid, and the taste and texture is unlike any other nut butter I find at the store. I always keep pumpkin seeds, hazelnuts, walnuts, pecans, and almonds on hand for nut milk and Power Protein Granola (page 84).

Condiments and Fermented Things

I cannot live without a jar of extra-strong Dijon mustard and a bottle of low-sodium tamari. I use these two ingredients in most of my sauces and dressings. When I'm not in the mood to cook, I'll wilt some greens and add olive oil and tamari, slice some raw goat cheese, and take a few olives from the pantry and put them all on a plate with a dollop of sharp Dijon mustard; it is truly heaven on a plate. I use tamari in just about everything, even tomato sauce, for its rich umami flavor. It's naturally gluten-free and a bit more mild than soy sauce, which is why I prefer it. When buying a Dijon, I try to find one that uses sea salt and omits any preservatives or sulfates. The best are always products of France, and my favorite is Trois Petits Cochons, which you can find at many specialty food stores or online. Rounding out my condiment collection are fruit-juice-sweetened strawberry and apricot jams; a good bottle of vegan mayonnaise for dressings, sandwiches, and much more; and a collection of fermented foods, like sauerkraut, miso paste, and apple cider vinegar, to brighten any dressing or dish.

Oils, Spices, and Herbs

I prepare food with three types of oils: extra-virgin olive oil for seasoning and dressing, and avocado and coconut oil for high-heat cooking. I also use ghee, a type of clarified butter, which is naturally lactose- and casein-free and rich in healthy fats and nutrients. Ghee can have a gamy flavor, but Ancient Organics makes a very mild one that I love.

As for spices, dried herbs, and seasonings, I don't believe you need an overflowing spice drawer to make great food. I return again and again to sea salt, cayenne pepper, freshly ground black peppercorns, paprika, turmeric, oregano, and curry powder. I look for spices and herbs that are nonirradiated and preservative-free; my favorite brand is Frontier Co-op. The recipes in this book are all tested with Himalayan pink salt or Redmond Real Salt; for flaky salt, my favorite is Maldon. While some of the recipes in this book call for black pepper (namely the dressings), I try to avoid it in my cooking and rarely use it to season food, as it is acidic and hard to digest. A little known fact is that while salt is essential to flavor, cooking with black pepper is not. In general, I prefer fresh herbs to dry ones, and you will always find big bunches of parsley, cilantro, chives, dill, and basil in my kitchen, which I buy year-round from the farmers' market.

Baking Essentials

A good gluten-free all-purpose flour is key. I love Arrowhead Mills Organic. I prefer to grind my own oat flour from whole rolled oats; One Degree Organics is my favorite brand, and it's certified glyphosate-free. When recipes call for almond flour, it is always whole almond flour, and I always use organic, non-GMO cornmeal for baked polenta and corn bread on chili night. I stick with unrefined and lower-glycemic sugars, such as coconut, date, and maple sugar, as well as maple, date, and brown-rice syrups, and pure vanilla paste or extract. I always have coconut sugar–sweetened chocolate and carob chips and a few bars of dark chocolate for baking, melting, and snacking. If you love a last-minute baking project like we do, be sure to stock some baking soda and aluminum-free baking powder as well.

Sweets and Snacks

When it comes to desserts and snacking, I try to avoid packaged and heavily processed foods, but in our busy world that's not always possible, so I wanted to give you a few options for better-for-you snacks that I always keep stocked. There are many wonderful brands in the packaged-food space, and also a lot of health-washing, so when I read labels, I try to choose snacks with as few ingredients as possible. I avoid highly inflammatory oils like canola and vegetable, and I look for sweets without refined sugars. We love roasted seaweed snacks cooked in avocado oil, chickpea puffs, gluten-free pretzels and seed crackers, jars of olives, and whole food bars or cookies sweetened with dates and coconut sugar.

Filtered Water

The recipes in this book call for filtered water. Most of us don't think about the water we drink, but water quality is foundational to our health. Tap water can contain industrial chemicals like fluoride, chlorine, and chromium-6. It can also host parasites, as well as contain traces of heavy metals. Bottled water is not much better; most is contaminated with lead, arsenic, and environmental pollutants, and it is usually sold in plastic bottles (we'll discuss in the following section how bad plastics are for our health and our environment). Choosing a good under-the-counter filter and using refillable water bottles is the most sustainable option. There are many ways to filter your water, but I like a high-quality carbon filter best, such as Multipure.

CREATING A NONTOXIC KITCHEN

How we cook is as important as what we cook. Let's talk about how to choose the right cookware and kitchen equipment for optimal health and well-being! By now we know that forever chemicals like plastics, PFOAs/PTFEs, lead, and industrial cleaning by-products are bad news. We also know that these chemicals have made their way into our homes and our food supply. The good news is that with a few mindful choices we can minimize our exposure to these toxins and keep them out of our kitchens!

Say Adios to Aluminum

- **HERE'S WHAT WE KNOW:** Aluminum is a heavy metal and a known neurotoxin. When it builds up in the bloodstream, it can cause a host of nasty health problems, like dementia and heavy-metal poisoning, but it is still widely used in cookware and bakeware and even baking powder! It's also the main component of everyone's favorite kitchen staple, aluminum foil.

- **HERE'S WHAT YOU CAN DO:** If you use aluminum foil, use a layer of parchment paper between the foil and the food. This way when you cook and store your food, the aluminum won't get absorbed into it. Another way to get rid of heavy metals in your kitchen is to buy stainless-steel, cast-iron, and nontoxic nonstick cookware. There are many brands that make affordable, durable, and sustainable options. My favorites for nonstick are GreenPan and Caraway Home. For stainless-steel cookware I use All-Clad, and for cast iron and enameled cast iron, Lodge, Le Creuset, and Staub. Enameled cast iron can be more expensive than other materials, but it lasts a long time, so you can invest in one or two pieces like a Dutch oven for soups and stews and a casserole dish for lasagnas or shepherd's pie, and you're good to go!

Peace Out, Plastic

- **HERE'S WHAT WE KNOW:** There's nothing safe about plastics. They are made of "forever chemicals" that interfere with gut health, our immune systems, and our hormones. Plastics have been found in amniotic fluid and cord blood, meaning babies are exposed to the negative effects of plastics before they are even born. Single-use plastics wind up in landfills and the ocean, posing a grave threat to the environment.

- **HERE'S WHAT YOU CAN DO:** Buy glass or food-grade silicone storage containers instead of plastic containers and bags. My favorites are Pyrex food storage containers for leftovers and Stasher silicone bags for storing snacks and other small items. Glass mason jars are readily available online and are great for storing nut milks, dressings, juices, and soups.

Nontoxic Pots, Pans, and Tools I Love

Contrary to what some home cooks may tell you, you don't need a ton of pots, pans, tools, and gadgets to cook great meals. You need just a few things, some more expensive than others, that are high-quality and made from nontoxic materials. If properly cared for, they will last a very long time.

For nonstick cookware that is PTFE- and PFOA-free, I love Caraway Home or GreenPan stainless-steel skillets and my All-Clad large pasta pot, and I opt for food-grade silicone and sustainably forested wood in lieu of plastic tools.

Here's a list of my most-used cookware and my favorite brands for each:

- 10-inch cast-iron skillet (Lodge or Staub)
- 8- and 10-inch nonstick skillets (Caraway Home, or GreenPan for a more affordable option)
- 6-quart stainless-steel pot (All-Clad)
- 15-quart enameled cast-iron Dutch oven (Le Creuset)
- Nontoxic bakeware set (Caraway Home or GreenPan), including rimmed baking sheets
- 9 × 13-inch ceramic or enameled cast-iron baking dish for lasagna and casseroles
- High-powered blender (Vitamix or Beast)
- Instant Pot (or pressure cooker)
- Tools: silicone and wooden spatulas and spoons, rasp grater (Microplane), sturdy vegetable peeler, salad spinner, cheese grater
- Knives: chef's knife for chopping vegetables, bread knife with a serrated blade, paring knife

VIDA
MISEN

Getting Started: A Few Essential Tips for Cooking Healthy and Wholesome Meals

We're almost ready to start cooking! Before we do, let's go over a few simple but essential methods for prepping, preparing, and enjoying natural and whole foods.

WASHING AND STORING PRODUCE

The easiest way to add more veggies to your diet is to spend thirty minutes at the beginning of the week washing, drying, and storing your produce. That way, when you want to whip up a stir-fry or a quick soup, the ingredients are all ready and waiting in the fridge. We talked about the benefits of choosing organic (page 12), but it's also important to make sure you are cleaning your produce properly. Here's my tried-and-true method:

1. Fill your sink with cold water, and add three drops of grapefruit seed extract or food-grade hydrogen peroxide. Place your fruit and veg in the water and allow them to soak for fifteen minutes. This removes any chemical residue or wax as well as bugs and food-borne pathogens. Drain and rinse your produce. For any leafy vegetables, like lettuce or kale, use a salad spinner to spin dry.

2. Lay clean dish towels on your counter and place your washed produce on them. Allow the fruit and vegetables to air-dry for about fifteen minutes, or until all the moisture is gone. Once dry, the produce will last much longer in the fridge.

3. Wrap any veggies that get refrigerated in recycled paper towels, place in a reusable produce bag, and store it in the fridge. Potatoes can be left on the counter in a bowl. For mushrooms, it is best to wait to wash until you are ready to use them, as they are prone to mold. Onions and garlic should also be washed immediately before using. Place any fruit like apples, pears, and oranges in a fruit bowl on the counter. For more fragile fruit that gets refrigerated, like blueberries and strawberries, place them in open glass containers lined with paper towels in the fridge. You might have to swap out the paper once or twice, but they will last up to five days in the fridge.

SOAKING, STEWING, AND STORING BEANS AND WHOLE GRAINS

Naturally gluten-free whole grains (like oats, quinoa, and jasmine rice) are a staple of my family's diet. If I'm ever stumped on what to prepare for dinner, I usually make a bowl of rice and beans with a load of healthy toppings like avocado, sauerkraut, and chopped veggies, and the whole family is happy. My kids have all gone through picky phases, but a bowl of rice and beans or oatmeal usually satisfies them. The best way to get the most out of grains and beans is to make sure they are prepared properly for optimal digestion. We all know the rhyme "Beans, beans, they're good for your heart, the more you eat, the more you . . ." Beans get a bad rap for causing gassiness, but if cooked the right way, they are very easy to digest.

Cooking Beans

Soak beans in cold water overnight, adding 3 cups of water for every 1 cup of beans, and leave them on the countertop covered. (Putting dried beans in the refrigerator makes them even harder to break down.) In the morning, drain and rinse the beans and pressure-cook them. Pressure-cooking your beans in an Instant Pot or pressure cooker cuts down the cooking time and destroys the lectins, making them very easy to digest. If you are trying to eat a more whole food and vegetarian diet, an Instant Pot is a wonderful investment. You can also cook your beans in a slow cooker or on the stovetop, but it takes much longer and they won't be as gentle on your stomach.

Cooking Grains

If you want to reap the benefits of naturally gluten-free whole grains, you need to soak them to break down the phytic acid in their hard outer shells and release their essential minerals and nutrients. I soak all grains in cold water, place them in the fridge covered overnight, drain and rinse in the morning, and cook on the stovetop. Soaking grains also reduces the cooking time, making them much easier to incorporate into everyday meals.

STORING GRAINS, LEGUMES, NUTS, AND SEEDS

Grains, legumes, nuts, and seeds have natural oils that can go rancid when exposed to heat and light. Rancid oils lead to free-radical damage in the body, which causes a whole host of nasty side effects, including premature aging. The best way to protect against rancid oil is to store your grains, legumes, nuts, and seeds in the freezer or fridge. They last longer, stay fresh, and taste delicious! Plus, you'll be doing your body good! Once you've tasted a jar of peanut butter with its oils intact, trust me, you'll never go back.

CHOOSING THE RIGHT OILS

Speaking of oils . . . not all oils are created equal. For the purpose of these recipes (and your overall well-being), you'll want to stick with organic, cold-pressed olive, coconut, and avocado oils. These oils are rich in omega-3 fatty acids and have the right ratio of omega-3 and omega-6 fats, meaning they are anti-inflammatory. When I'm using high heat (that is, stir-frying, sautéing, and scrambling), I stick with avocado oil. When I'm roasting or baking, I love the rich, sweet, and nutty flavor of coconut oil, especially for things like roasted squash and banana bread. I save extra-virgin olive oil for finishing dishes, making salad dressings, and drizzling on soup and hummus.

USING LEFTOVERS

If you live alone, work long hours, or you are just getting started on this path of heathy eating, you might be wondering how to use these principles in a way that works for you. One of the benefits of prepping and cooking this way is that you will always have a well-stocked fridge and can easily repurpose leftovers into healthy meals. Pressure-cooked beans stay good in the fridge for four or five days if kept in some reserved cooking liquid and stored in an airtight container. The same goes for grains. In the following chapters, I'll teach you how to make wonderful meals and fan favorites like quick black bean quesadillas, zucchini and goat cheese, tofu stir-fries, and easy one-pot stews using leftovers. There is nothing more satisfying than having friends over for an impromptu healthy dinner or making a home-cooked meal at the end of a long day, even though you might be tempted to order in.

MEAL PREP MAGIC

Sauces, Dips & Dressings

Ginger-Tamari Dressing, 32

If You Love Mustard Vinaigrette, 33

Health Food Café–Style Tahini Dressing

Health Food Café–Style Tahini Dressing

Back in the '90s in New York City, there were only a few organic and vegetarian restaurants. My two favorites were Souen and Angelica Kitchen, and both had the most delicious hippie-style tahini dressing. Angelica's was straight-up classic, while Souen's was extra heavy on the tahini, dotted with fresh dill, and blended with silken tofu to make it even creamier. Both were heavenly. I drizzled them on everything from steamed squash and broccoli to pasta. This recipe is my homage to Angelica and Souen. It's a bit thicker than the traditional tahini you find at Middle Eastern restaurants, but it hits home for me. This is also the tahini we serve at Spring Café Aspen with our beloved falafel wrap.

MAKES 2 CUPS

1 cup **tahini**

Juice of 1 **lemon**

½ teaspoon **fine sea salt**

½ cup plus 3 tablespoons **ice water**

¼ cup chopped **fresh dill**

1. In a medium bowl, whisk together the tahini, lemon juice, salt, and ice water until fully incorporated and smooth. Fold in the dill.

2. The dressing can be stored in an airtight container in the refrigerator for up to 2 weeks.

Ginger–Tamari Dressing

Pungent ginger and salty, umami tamari make the most perfect flavor combo in my humble opinion. This dressing also has balsamic for a little hit of acidity and apple juice to round it all out. Sometimes if I'm making it as a marinade, I'll use freshly juiced apples, but you can easily buy the apple juice at a store. You can find ginger juice at most health food stores. This sauce brings out the best in any vegetable. You can use it as a marinade for tofu or to liven up a simple bowl of steamed rice or quinoa. I've even used this dressing as a sauce for a noodle or vegetable stir-fry. It comes together in minutes and keeps nicely in the fridge so you can make it ahead of time and then use it to enhance your weeknight meals.

MAKES ABOUT 2 CUPS

1 cup low-sodium **tamari**

¼ cup **balsamic vinegar**

¼ cup **ginger juice**

2 tablespoons **toasted sesame oil**

Juice of 1 **lemon**

2 tablespoons **apple juice**

⅛ teaspoon **fine sea salt**

1. In a medium bowl, whisk together the tamari, balsamic vinegar, ginger juice, sesame oil, lemon juice, apple juice, and salt until fully emulsified.

2. The dressing can be stored in an airtight container in the refrigerator for up to 2 weeks.

If You Love Mustard Vinaigrette

When I was studying abroad in Paris there was a brasserie down the street from the university. We used to duck out of afternoon classes just in time to sit for a salad and fries (yes, as a college student in France, I ate a lot of fries). The salad came with the most perfect mustard vinaigrette I've ever eaten—briny and tart enough to clear your sinuses but so smooth it almost appeared whipped. I dream of that vinaigrette, and this is my version. It works well with anything, but I love to get a small bunch of little gems from the farmers' market and slather it on top. Any type of Dijon mustard will do, but if you can get your hands on a jar of strong Dijon, even better!

MAKES ABOUT 2 CUPS

6 tablespoons **Dijon mustard**

Juice of 2 **lemons**

1 cup **extra-virgin olive oil**

1 teaspoon **fine sea salt**

Freshly ground **black pepper**

1. In a medium bowl, whisk together the mustard, lemon juice, olive oil, salt, and pepper until fully emulsified.

2. The dressing can be stored in an airtight container in the refrigerator for up to 2 weeks.

The Perfect Salad Dressing

I would call this recipe our "house dressing," meaning it's my go-to salad dressing for most days of the week. It's acidic without being sharp, mild without being too sweet, a little tangy from the mustard, and it works with just about any type of salad. This is a great starter recipe if you're looking to switch from store-bought dressing to homemade. The ingredients are approachable, and you can keep it in a mason jar in the fridge and use it all week. I call it the Perfect Salad Dressing, but really, it's the perfect universal dressing, meaning you could drizzle some on a bowl of quinoa and roasted squash and it would do the trick.

MAKES ABOUT 2 CUPS

Juice of 2 **lemons**

¼ cup **apple cider vinegar**

1 tablespoon **Dijon mustard**

2 teaspoons **pure maple syrup**

2 teaspoons **dried oregano**

½ teaspoon **fine sea salt**

Freshly ground **black pepper**

1 cup **extra-virgin olive oil**

1. In a medium bowl, whisk together the lemon juice, apple cider vinegar, mustard, maple syrup, oregano, salt, some pepper, and olive oil until fully emulsified.

2. The dressing can be stored in an airtight container in the refrigerator for up to 2 weeks.

Herby Balsamic Vinaigrette, 37
The Perfect Salad Dressing
Secret Sauce, 36

Secret Sauce

This is a very basic recipe with a very big reward. When I was growing up, my mom would often make homemade veggie burgers, with rice-and-bean burgers, buns, and all the fixings. I've always loved the idea of a burger—not so much for the patty as for the soft white bun, the melted cheese, the side of fries, and the pinkish sauce that you only see around a burger. When I left home for college, I subsisted on a lot of veggie burgers and bags of frozen organic crinkle fries, but I always craved that pinkish secret sauce. One day I came up with this recipe and never looked back. It tastes exactly like what I imagine real burger-joint sauce tastes like.

MAKES ABOUT 1½ CUPS

1 cup **vegan mayo**, such as Vegenaise

½ cup **ketchup**

½ teaspoon **onion powder**

½ teaspoon **garlic powder**

½ teaspoon **fine sea salt**

1. In a medium bowl, whisk together the mayo, ketchup, onion powder, garlic powder, and salt until fully combined.

2. The sauce can be stored in an airtight container in the refrigerator for up to 2 weeks.

Herby Balsamic Vinaigrette

I love fresh herbs in a salad dressing, especially when paired with acidic, sweet balsamic and lots of fresh lemon juice. I make this recipe a lot in the summer, when thyme, sage, and parsley abound in my garden. Pour it over chopped tomatoes or crisp romaine lettuce, and there is really nothing better.

MAKES 1½ CUPS

½ cup **extra-virgin olive oil**

½ cup **balsamic vinegar**

2 tablespoons chopped **fresh sage**

2 tablespoons chopped **fresh thyme leaves**

2 tablespoons chopped **fresh flat-leaf parsley**

¼ teaspoon **fine sea salt**

Freshly **cracked black pepper**

Juice of 2 **lemons**

1. In a medium bowl, whisk together the olive oil, balsamic vinegar, sage, thyme, parsley, salt, some pepper, and lemon juice. Add 2 tablespoons water and whisk until fully emulsified.

2. The dressing can be stored in an airtight container in the refrigerator for up to 2 weeks.

Go-to Guacamole

I call this "Go-to Guacamole" because I've discovered that kids will eat almost anything if they can dip it in this. I like to make a batch and do a big, beautiful board with crudités, chips, and raw goat cheese for the kids when they get home from school. I favor my guac chunky and heavy on the cilantro and lime juice. Because avocados are loaded with healthy fats and plant protein, I feel great about everyone filling up on guac.

SERVES 4 TO 6

4 or 5 ripe **avocados**

Juice of 2 **limes**

1 teaspoon **fine sea salt**, plus more as needed

2 small **plum** or **hothouse tomatoes**, diced

½ bunch **cilantro**, chopped

1 teaspoon **smoked paprika**

Assorted crudités and/or **tortilla chips**, such as Siete Grain Free Tortilla Chips, for serving

1. Halve each avocado lengthwise and remove the pits. Using a large spoon, scoop out the flesh from both sides of each avocado and place in a large bowl. Using the spoon or a fork, mash the avocado flesh. Stir in the lime juice and season with the salt.

2. Add the tomatoes, cilantro, and paprika. Stir again to combine and taste for seasoning, adding more salt, if needed. Serve immediately, with crudités and/or chips alongside for dipping.

NOTE: Guacamole is best served as soon as possible after it's made, but if you need to make it in advance, place a piece of parchment directly on the top of the guacamole mixture to create a seal and then cover with a lid. The guacamole will keep in the refrigerator for up to 6 hours.

Pico de Gallo

Whenever I don't know what to make for dinner, I always make Mexican food. It's easy to prepare for a large group. My kids devour it, my husband is happy, and I never tire of it. Tacos, burritos, enchiladas, or anything wrapped in a tortilla is a great way to pack in loads of plants, flavors, and textures. Blanca, our founding chef from Spring Café in Aspen, taught me this pico recipe years ago when we first opened our doors, and it remains my favorite: perfectly salty, tangy, and fresh. I of course make it on Mexican night, but my favorite way to enjoy it is with avocado toast or eggs for breakfast.

MAKES 3 CUPS

4 **beefsteak tomatoes**, diced

½ large **white onion**, diced

Juice of 2 **limes**

¾ teaspoon **fine sea salt**, plus more to taste

½ bunch **cilantro**, chopped

1. In a large bowl, combine the tomatoes, onion, lime juice, and salt. Fold in the cilantro and taste for seasoning.

2. Serve cold or at room temperature. Pico will keep in an airtight container in the refrigerator for up to 3 days.

Cilantro Coconut Crema

I developed this recipe so that my dairy-sensitive family could enjoy a delicious crema on Taco Tuesday, which is our favorite night of the week. If you use a mild coconut yogurt, this sauce tastes nothing like coconut, I promise. The secret is the garlic and onion powders and the freshly chopped cilantro. This is also excellent if you are making a taco salad or simply want to enjoy a bowl of rice and beans. If I'm entertaining and doing a Mexican theme for the evening, I'll make a dip trio with Go-to Guacamole (page 39), Pico de Gallo (page 40), and this crema, and everyone always goes wild for it.

MAKES 1½ CUPS

1 cup unsweetened **coconut yogurt**

¼ cup **extra-virgin olive oil**

¼ cup chopped **fresh cilantro**

Juice of 2 **limes**

¼ teaspoon **onion powder**

¼ teaspoon **garlic powder**

⅛ teaspoon **fine sea salt**

1. In a small bowl, whisk together the coconut yogurt, olive oil, cilantro, lime juice, onion powder, garlic powder, and salt until smooth and all the ingredients are fully incorporated.
2. The crema can be stored in an airtight container in the refrigerator for up to 1 week.

Slow-Roasted Chunky Tomato Sauce

You can turn any tomato into a perfect tomato by slow-roasting it—a trick that is particularly handy when it's not peak tomato season. I love to make this sauce on cold winter nights and serve it over heaping bowls of brown-rice pasta with a side of garlic bread. The sauce also makes a lovely addition to warm grain dishes, egg scrambles, or hearty sandwiches. You can also skip the pulsing step and just keep the roasted tomatoes and garlic in an airtight jar in the fridge, to use as a condiment on grains and egg and tofu dishes.

MAKES 4 CUPS

16 **plum tomatoes**

4 or 5 **garlic cloves**, peeled

3 to 4 tablespoons **extra-virgin olive oil**

1 tablespoon **fine sea salt**, plus more to taste

1. Preheat the oven to 325°F.

2. Using a chef's knife, chop the tomatoes into 1-inch pieces and scatter on a baking sheet. Evenly distribute the garlic cloves, drizzle everything with the olive oil, and season with the salt.

3. Roast the tomatoes and garlic for 90 minutes, stirring every 20 to 30 minutes, until the tomatoes are bright red and their juices have thickened and are jammy. Remove the tomatoes and garlic from the oven and allow them to cool for 10 minutes.

4. Place the cooled tomatoes and garlic in a food processor or blender. Pulse until a chunky sauce forms. Taste for seasoning and more salt, if necessary.

5. The sauce can be stored in an airtight container in the refrigerator for up to 2 weeks or in the freezer for up to 3 months.

Juices & Drinks

Good Morning Green

I think about my morning juice the way most people think about their morning coffee. It's my nonnegotiable ritual. But as much as I love things that are good for me, I also love food and drinks that taste great, and this juice checks both boxes. It's tangy and perfectly sweet from the combo of lemon and green apple, and the hint of fennel really helps digest anything left over from the night before! Think of this as your gateway to green juice; try it and you won't look back. If you want a more savory juice, omit the green apple and add another dark-leaf green like bok choy or dandelion greens or simply add more celery or cucumber.

MAKES 32 OUNCES; SERVES 4

8 **celery stalks**

1 bunch **lacinato kale** (12 or 13 leaves)

1 head **romaine lettuce**

2 small **fennel bulbs**

1 large **Persian cucumber**

1 small **green apple**, such as Granny Smith

1 **lemon**

½ cup **fresh cilantro**

Add the celery to the juicer whole. Coarsely chop the kale and romaine and cut the fennel and cucumber in half. Core the apple. Remove and discard the rind from the lemon. Add the kale, romaine, fennel, cucumber, apple, and lemon to the juicer along with the cilantro. (This juice can be made up to 1 day in advance and stored in the refrigerator.)

Tangy Tang

I make this juice all summer long. It's refreshing, hydrating, and full of nutrients but sweet enough that the kids think it tastes like fruit punch. This is a great juice to start with if you're dipping your toe into juicing; you can easily add 3 to 4 stalks of celery to get a little green in.

MAKES 16 OUNCES; SERVES 2

1 **cantaloupe**

1 **pineapple**

2 **limes**

1 (1-inch) piece **fresh ginger**

1. Using a chef's knife, remove the top and the bottom of the cantaloupe. Sit the cantaloupe on one of its ends and, using your knife, cut between the flesh and the skin from top to bottom, removing the skin along all the sides of the fruit. Cut in half and remove the seeds. Chop into 1- to 2-inch pieces.

2. Repeat the same process to remove the skin of the pineapple. Cut around the interior core and discard. Cut the pineapple into 2-inch pieces.

3. Remove the rind from the limes and peel the ginger.

4. Add the cantaloupe, pineapple, limes, and ginger to the juicer. (This juice can be made up to 1 day in advance and stored in the refrigerator.)

Beet Mine Forever

Beets are nature's aspirin; they are high in nitrate and they oxygenate the blood. This is my go-to recipe all winter when I need something warming and grounding but still want an invigorating taste. Beets are earthy, so I like to pair them with bright fruits like pineapple or watermelon and lots of lime. If you want an extra kick, just add a touch of grated ginger or fresh turmeric.

MAKES 32 OUNCES; SERVES 4

2 pounds **red beets** (9 or 10 medium beets)

1 **pineapple**

1 **lime**

1. Scrub the beets and cut them in half, as needed, to fit into the juicer. Remove the top and bottom of the pineapple. Sit the pineapple on one of its ends and, using a chef's knife, cut between the flesh and the skin from top to bottom, removing the skin along all the sides of the fruit. Cut around the interior core and discard. Cut the pineapple into 2-inch pieces. Remove the rind from the lime.

2. Place the beets, pineapple, and lime into the juicer. (This juice can be made up to 1 day in advance and stored in the refrigerator.)

PRO TIP: I love to drink this juice when I'm at a higher elevation and need extra oxygen, or when I have a headache. For all my ladies, it's extra beneficial during *that time of the month*!

Let's Talk Juicing

Juice can be made either in a centrifugal juicer (such as most countertop models) or in a cold press (like the bottles you see in most grab-and-go juice concepts). The easiest way to drink juice daily at home is to acquire a centrifugal juicer. My favorites are:

- **MAGIC BULLET MINI JUICER:** $ (great for small countertops and for travel)
- **BREVILLE JUICE FOUNTAIN:** $$ (a fast and easy-to-clean home option if you have a little bit more space)
- **OMEGA JUICER:** $$$ (slower and a little more luxe, but makes delicious soft serve and nut butters as well)

Before you begin juicing, there a few simple steps to follow:

- **USE ORGANIC PRODUCE.** Juice lacks fiber, so it's instantly digested and absorbed into the body and bloodstream. Juice made with conventional produce is like taking a shot of pesticides right to the gut. Don't bother!
- **WASH ALL THE VEGGIES AND FRUIT FIRST.** I know what you're thinking: "It takes so much time and effort! How will I ever do it?" I promise, you can do it!
- **DRINK YOUR JUICE FIRST THING IN THE MORNING ON AN EMPTY STOMACH** (before coffee, if you can manage it). Why? Fresh vegetable juice is the most alkaline thing we can put in our bodies. Alkalinity equals health, and acidity equals disease. Prepping your body with something alkaline first thing in the morning gives you a great foundation for the rest of your day.

THE JUICY DETAILS ON HOW TO GET JUICING

- Whenever you do your weekly grocery shop, stock up on these things: 1 extra bag of carrots, 1 extra head of celery, 2 heads of romaine, 1 head of kale, 5 cucumbers, and 5 apples (all this will be good for 5 to 6 days). Dedicate 20 minutes after you get home to wash and dry your produce (see page 25).
- First thing in the morning when you get to the kitchen, pull out your prewashed produce, run it through the juicer, and drink it down! If you follow the recipes in this book, you'll have enough for 2 to 4 people, and since centrifugal juice needs to be drunk right away to get the most out of the nutrients, you don't have to worry about making a large batch and storing it. Just shop, wash, juice, and drink!

Immunity Juice

For most of my childhood, my mom would wake me up with a freshly juiced carrot, apple, and orange drink that I would down before breakfast. It was sweet, tangy, and delicious, and best of all, it was orange, which I thought was the coolest thing ever at the time. I drank so much carrot juice as a kid that I had a permanent carrot juice mustache. One day in elementary school our French teacher pulled me aside and asked me why my lips were always stained orange when I came to school. I told her it must be from the carrot juice my mom made for me, and she gave me a puzzled look. Horrified, she said, "You drink juice from carrots?" Later that day she pulled my mom aside at pickup and shared her deep concern and dismay. She said something along the lines of "You're raising a child, not a bunny." Watching my mom try to explain the virtues of freshly pressed carrot juice to my elementary French teacher is something we laugh about to this day. I gave all my boys this juice when they started solids, and it's the best immune-boosting cure-all when you feel tired, sick, or a little run-down. My kids call it "juicy juice" because it's just so bright and thirst-quenching and, well, juicy.

MAKES 32 OUNCES; SERVES 4

2½ pounds **carrots** (about 11 medium to large carrots)

2 **navel oranges**

1 **lemon**

1 (1-inch) piece **fresh ginger**

1 (1-inch) piece **fresh turmeric**

1. Peel the carrots and remove the rind from the oranges and lemon. Peel the ginger.

2. Place the carrots, oranges, lemon, ginger, and turmeric in the juicer. (This juice can be made up to 1 day in advance and stored in the refrigerator.)

pyrex
1000 ml
1 litre
900 ml
800 ml
700 ml
500 ml
300 ml

The Cleanser

I make this juice when I'm craving something light and refreshing—and only have a few moments before rushing out the door. It's also great for the morning after an extra-heavy meal, or if you just feel off and need to reboot and re-center. Celery juice is highly alkaline and anti-inflammatory but easy to drink. The pineapple adds a hint of sweetness (you could substitute green apple here), while ginger and lime give it a tangy boost. This is a lovely recipe if you're just starting to flirt with juicing and dark leafy greens don't appeal to you so early in the morning.

MAKES 16 OUNCES; SERVES 2

3 **celery stalks**

2 cups **baby spinach**

1 large **cucumber**

1 cup chopped **fresh pineapple**

1 (1-inch) piece **fresh ginger**, peeled

½ **lemon**

½ cup **fresh flat-leaf parsley**

Juice the celery whole with the spinach. Cut the cucumber in half and add to the juicer, followed by the pineapple and ginger. Remove the rind from the lemon and add to the juicer with the parsley. (This juice can be made up to 1 day in advance and stored in the refrigerator.)

Throat Saver

While not a juice, this drink is very healing, and I like to drink it on colder mornings, especially if I'm under the weather. This recipe is inspired by an immunity tonic that our wonderful caregiver, Gaga, lovingly makes for me and the boys whenever we get sick. It's strong but incredibly healing and soothing. I modified the amount of ginger to make it more user-friendly, but feel free to add as much as you can tolerate. Make sure you use manuka honey for its natural antimicrobial properties and throat-soothing goodness.

SERVES 1

2 to 3 ounces **fresh ginger**, peeled and sliced

Juice of 1 **orange**

Juice of ½ **lemon**

½ teaspoon **manuka honey**, or to taste

1. In a small saucepan, combine 2 cups water and the ginger and bring to a boil over medium-high heat. Remove the pan from the heat and allow the mixture to steep for 5 minutes. Use a slotted spoon to remove the ginger and reserve it for another use.

2. Pour the orange and lemon juices into a mug. Pour the hot ginger water into the mug and stir in the honey. Serve hot.

Smoothies

Peanut Butter Berry Blast

When my oldest son turned seven, he started to get interested in what I was doing in the kitchen. One morning I woke up and was alarmed to hear the blender running. I ran to the kitchen and found him pouring a smoothie he'd just made into cups for himself and his two younger brothers. He proudly told me the ingredients and dubbed it the Peanut Butter Berry Blast. He still makes it almost daily, and in my very biased opinion, it is delicious. It's also packed with protein from peanut butter and antioxidants from the frozen blueberries, making it a great breakfast smoothie.

MAKES 16 OUNCES; SERVES 2

1 frozen peeled **banana**

4 **strawberries**, hulled

1 cup **blueberries**

1 tablespoon creamy **peanut butter**

10 ounces unsweetened **almond milk**

In a high-speed blender or food processor, blend the banana, strawberries, blueberries, peanut butter, and almond milk until the mixture is smooth and thick. Serve cold immediately.

The Green Banana

If I had to pick a favorite smoothie, this would be it. I love to use Asian greens like tatsoi and bok choy in green smoothies; you get all the benefits of dark leafy greens like spinach and kale, but the Asian greens have a milder taste and are easier to digest raw. I make this smoothie on mornings when I feel like I need more than a green juice to start my day but still want something nutritious and clean. The spirulina is an excellent source of plant protein and gives a gorgeous green hue.

MAKES 8 OUNCES; SERVES 1

1 frozen peeled **banana**

1 head **baby tatsoi** or **baby bok choy** (about 1½ cups)

¼ cup unsweetened **almond milk**

1 tablespoon **spirulina**

In a high-speed blender or food processor, blend the banana, tatsoi, almond milk, and spirulina until creamy and smooth. Serve cold immediately.

Coco Mango

This smoothie reminds me of the thick, sweet mango lassis I drank throughout India, but with the added twist of coconut and ginger. Coconut milk is probiotic-rich and filled with healthy fats, so this smoothie is my go-to when I need something filling and nourishing. The fresh ginger cuts a bit of the sweetness and is also wonderful for digestion and an immunity boost. If you want it a bit lighter, you can use all coconut water instead of coconut milk. In the summer I like to take extra-ripe mangoes and cut them in chunks and freeze them, but if you're like me and you crave a taste of the tropics all winter long, store-bought frozen organic mango will do just fine in this recipe.

MAKES 16 OUNCES; SERVES 2

- 1 cup frozen chopped **mango**
- 1 frozen peeled **banana**
- ⅓ cup canned unsweetened full-fat **coconut milk**
- 1 cup unsweetened **coconut water**
- 1 (1-inch) piece **fresh ginger**, peeled

In a high-speed blender or food processor, blend the mango, banana, coconut milk, coconut water, and ginger until thick and creamy. Serve cold immediately.

Piña Colada Smoothie

This smoothie reminds me of the beach vacations I used to take with my parents as a kid. The hotels we visited always had virgin piña coladas and strawberry daiquiris from a powdered mix, and once in a while my mom would let me order them on the beach for a treat. This smoothie has the same delicious fruity taste but none of the artificial flavor or color. Normally, I like a creamy smoothie, but this one borders on slushy to give it the right feel. My kids drink them all summer long, and I like to make a big batch for pool parties and other gatherings; adults love them too. If you want to get creative with your presentation, add a wedge of pineapple or an orange slice to the side of the glass.

MAKES 16 OUNCES; SERVES 2

1 cup frozen **pineapple chunks**

1 cup (about 8 ounces) chopped frozen **raw coconut meat**

1 cup unsweetened **coconut water**

½ cup unsweetened **almond milk**

Pineapple wedges or **orange slices**, for garnish (optional)

In a high-speed blender or food processor, blend the pineapple, coconut meat, coconut water, and almond milk until thick and creamy. Garnish each serving with a pineapple wedge or orange slice, if using. Serve cold immediately.

Malteds

My mom used to bring me malteds after school as a special treat before sporting activities. A malted is a thick, creamy milkshake, usually made with malted milk powder. In these recipes, ingredients like frozen bananas, rich tahini, dates, and almond butter mimic the flavor and consistency of malted milk but allow you to make the smoothies dairy-free, alkaline, and still delicious. Carob is naturally sweet and doesn't have caffeine, making it an excellent alternative to chocolate, especially later in the day or for young kids. Malteds are one step closer to dessert than a smoothie, but these are so healthy you can enjoy them any time of the day! I make these for my kids after school because malteds are sweet but also nutrient- and protein-rich. If you have a sweet tooth but don't want something too sugary, try them for dessert. I like to serve them in tall glasses with long spoons, the kind you find in old-school diners, for a special retro touch.

TAHINI CAROB MALTED

MAKES 16 OUNCES; SERVES 2

3 pitted Medjool dates

1 frozen peeled banana

2 tablespoons tahini paste

1 tablespoon carob powder

1 cup unsweetened soy or oat milk

In a high-speed blender or food processor, blend the dates, banana, tahini paste, carob powder, and soy milk until thick and creamy. Serve immediately, while cold.

BANANA DATE CARAMEL MALTED

MAKES 16 OUNCES; SERVES 2

2 frozen peeled bananas

4 pitted Medjool dates

2 tablespoons almond butter

2 teaspoons pure vanilla extract

½ cup unsweetened soy or full-fat coconut milk

In a high-speed blender or food processor, blend the bananas, dates, almond butter, vanilla, and soy milk until thick and creamy. Serve immediately, while cold.

Mint Chip Shake

WITH COCONUT WHIP AND CHOCOLATE DRIZZLE

I'm not the biggest fan of mint chip ice cream, but I've always loved a mint chip milkshake. This one gets its vibrant color and flavor from spinach and peppermint extract. Whenever I serve this to guests, they go wild for it. It's decadent, perfectly minty, and gorgeous with the whipped coconut cream on top. The original inspiration for this recipe came from Pure Food and Wine, one of my favorite OG raw and vegetarian restaurants in New York City that closed many years ago. I still dream of their mint chip milkshake, and this one hits the spot.

MAKES 8 OUNCES; SERVES 1

2 pitted **Medjool dates**

1 cup **baby spinach**

½ ripe **banana**, peeled

½ ripe **avocado**

¼ cup unsweetened **almond milk**

1 tablespoon plus 1 teaspoon **pure maple syrup**

¼ teaspoon **pure peppermint extract**

1 cup plus 1 tablespoon **chocolate** or **vegan chocolate chips**, plus more for garnish

¼ cup cold unsweetened full-fat **coconut milk solids**

1. In a food processor or high-speed blender, blend the dates, spinach, banana, avocado, almond milk, 1 tablespoon of the maple syrup, the peppermint extract, 1 cup ice, and 1 tablespoon chocolate chips until the mixture is frothy and thick, like a shake.

2. To make the whipped coconut cream, take the solidified portion (about ¼ cup per can) of the coconut milk and place it in a large bowl with the remaining 1 teaspoon maple syrup. Using a hand or stand mixer, beat the coconut milk and maple syrup together until fluffy and resembling the texture of whipped cream, about 2 minutes.

3. Melt the remaining 1 cup chocolate chips in a double boiler or in a heatproof bowl sitting over a pot of boiling water (make sure the bottom of the bowl doesn't touch the water). While the sauce is warm, drizzle half of the sauce along the insides of your serving glass, twirling as needed to distribute.

4. Pour the shake into the glass and top with the whipped coconut cream. Garnish with the remaining chocolate sauce and additional chocolate chips. Serve cold immediately.

Coco Peanut

This is one of our more popular recipes at Spring Café Aspen, and I frequently make them at home. It's basically a peanut butter chocolate cup in smoothie form. I love to drink this when I have a chocolate craving, and the kids love them for a sweet treat as well. Sometimes in the summer I'll add a scoop of vegan coconut ice cream on top.

MAKES 16 OUNCES; SERVES 2

2 frozen peeled **bananas**

1 tablespoon **chia seeds**

1 tablespoon **cacao powder**

1 tablespoon creamy **peanut butter**

10 ounces unsweetened **almond milk**

In a high-speed blender or food processor, blend the banana, chia seeds, cacao powder, peanut butter, and almond milk until the mixture is smooth and thick. Serve cold immediately.

Tips for Making the Perfect Smoothie

FROZEN FRUIT, NEVER ICE

We all dream about the perfect thick, creamy smoothie. The secret? Frozen fruit, not ice! Ice makes smoothies that are watery and lacking the thick consistency we're striving for. Frozen peeled overripe bananas are the base of most of my smoothies. If you want a less sweet option, you can use frozen avocado or frozen coconut meat (available in most health food stores). I freeze fruit like berries and cut-up mangoes or buy frozen organic options and use them in my smoothie recipes. During colder months, or if I simply want a smoothie that's a little less cold, I use frozen bananas and fresh fruit. This gives the smoothie a thick consistency but brings the temp up just a bit. My kids don't love very cold smoothies, so this is a trick I use for them.

CHOOSING A LIQUID: WATER, COCONUT WATER, OR MILK

I like to make most smoothies with homemade nut milk or other plant-based milk, which gives them a creamy texture and makes them feel more like a meal. If you want a lighter consistency, try raw coconut water, which will lend a touch of sweetness and keep the smoothie extra refreshing. I especially like to use coconut water in green smoothies or summer-berry smoothies. You can absolutely make any of these recipes with filtered water; they won't be as creamy or sweet, but they will be just as delicious.

EXTRA CREDIT: PROTEIN, HEALTHY FATS, AND BROCCOLI SPROUTS

I tend to keep my smoothies pure and simple, but sometimes I want to add protein for an added boost. I don't love protein powders, but I often will add a scoop of nut butter (walnut, almond, or peanut) or a scoop of spirulina (an excellent source of plant protein) to my smoothies, especially if I'm taking one on the go during a busy morning or drinking it before a workout. If you need some extra protein, feel free to add nut butter or spirulina or even your favorite protein powder to any of these recipes. Healthy fats like organic coconut yogurt are also a great way to boost your smoothies and can be added to any recipe. If you want to transform a simple smoothie into a nutritional powerhouse, add broccoli sprouts; they are filled with sulforaphane, which is highly anticarcinogenic. The sprouts need to be broken up to release the sulforaphane, so putting them in a smoothie is a great way to include them in your diet. I add them for the whole family and feel good knowing my kids are reaping the benefits of the sprouts' cancer-fighting properties.

Breakfasts

Easy-as-Sliced-Bread French Toast

I can never decide if I'm a sweet or savory breakfast person. I love pancakes and French toast but don't want to feel like I've just eaten a massive sugar bomb to start my day. With this French toast, you get all the luxury of the classic but much less of the sugar (and you can skip the syrup if you want to keep it completely sugar-free). It really hits the spot without being too sweet or decadent. You can easily make it vegan by substituting a flax egg; if you do, just use a thicker vegan milk like oat or soy. Sometimes I even add crushed nuts to the batter for a little texture and crunch. My kids love this recipe and ask for it almost every morning, so I slather on some nut butter, cut some strawberries, and drizzle on a touch of date syrup, and they always devour their whole plate. If you're making a weekend brunch for family or friends, you could serve this with Hippie Dippy Scrambled Tofu (page 88) and Diner-Style Home Fries (page 96) for my absolute dream spread.

SERVES 4 TO 6

2 large **eggs**

1 cup unsweetened **almond milk**

¼ teaspoon **ground cinnamon**

1 teaspoon **pure vanilla extract**

1 heaping tablespoon smooth **walnut butter**

1 to 3 tablespoons **coconut oil**, for cooking

8 slices of your favorite **sandwich bread**, such as Sami's Bakery gluten-free bread

For Serving (Optional)

Grass-fed **butter**

Nut butter, at room temperature

Berries, sliced if large

Pure maple syrup or **date syrup**

1. In a shallow dish, crack the eggs and whisk until beaten. Add the milk, cinnamon, and vanilla and whisk to combine. Add the nut butter and, using a fork, gently stir until combined.

2. In a large nonstick skillet or on a large griddle, melt the coconut oil over medium heat.

3. When the oil is melted and glistening, dunk one slice of bread into the egg mixture, dipping as needed to make sure the slice is fully coated. (If using gluten-free bread, dip for only a moment until just coated.) Place the coated bread slice into the pan. Repeat the dunking with another slice of bread and add it to the pan, making sure that the pieces don't overlap. Cook for 1 to 2 minutes, then flip and cook until golden brown on the second side. Transfer to a plate and repeat with the remaining bread, adding more oil to the pan between batches as needed.

4. Serve immediately, with your choice of toppings.

The Fluffiest Gluten-Free Pancakes

When I had sleepovers at my best friend Karina's house as a kid, in the morning her mom would make these big pillowy, fluffy pancakes with white flour, sugar, butter, baking soda, milk, and eggs. I watched in wonder as she flipped them and marveled that something so simple could be so delicious. I'd devour an entire stack and then go home and ask my mom if she could please make pancakes like Karina's mom, but the answer was always a resounding no. To be fair, my mom made a mean pancake, but there is only so much almond flour and millet flour can do, am I right, people? While I will always eat gluten and dairy for pancakes (I love them that much!), with this recipe, I don't have to. I've been perfecting it for a long time, and I stand by these pancakes as the closest I've come to Karina's mom's. These freeze well, and you can batch cook them and heat them up in the toaster oven on busy weekday mornings.

MAKES 8 LARGE OR 16 SMALL PANCAKES

1 cup **gluten-free all-purpose flour** (see Notes)

¼ cup **almond flour**

1 teaspoon **baking powder**

1 teaspoon **baking soda**

1 cup unsweetened **oat milk**

1 teaspoon **pure vanilla extract**

1 tablespoon **pure maple syrup**, plus more for serving

1 large **egg**

Coconut oil, for cooking

Fruit, for serving (optional)

1. In a large bowl, whisk together the all-purpose flour, almond flour, baking powder, and baking soda. Add the oat milk, vanilla, maple syrup, and egg and whisk again until combined. Don't overwhisk; there will be some lumps.

2. Melt 1 tablespoon of coconut oil in a large nonstick skillet or large griddle over medium heat. When the oil is glistening, use a ¼-cup measure to spoon the batter onto the skillet, making as many pancakes as the space allows without overcrowding. Cook until bubbles form on the top of each pancake, 2 to 3 minutes. (Gluten-free pancakes have denser flour blends and don't cook as quickly as a regular all-purpose flour pancake would. Make sure you see a lot of air bubbles before you flip, or you'll wind up with undercooked, doughy pancakes.) Flip the pancakes and cook for 1 minute more. Remove the finished pancakes to a plate and repeat the process with the remaining batter, adding additional tablespoons of coconut oil as needed to prevent the batter from sticking.

3. Serve while warm with additional maple syrup and/or fruit.

NOTES

- If using a flour with xanthan gum, you will need to add an additional 1 cup oat milk.
- Use plenty of coconut oil or ghee in the pan; that's how you get that perfectly golden exterior.
- If you want to add blueberries (which we often do), add a few to each pancake *after* most of the air bubbles have formed and before you flip the pancakes; otherwise, the dough around the fruit won't cook fully.

Power Protein Granola

Granola is one of those foods I never loved until I started making my own. I find most store-bought granolas to be dry and full of added sugars—not a food I'd be pushing for breakfast. Enter Power Protein Granola. It's a perfect mix of chewy and crunchy, only mildly sweetened with maple syrup, perfectly crunchy but not dried out thanks to the coconut oil, and packed with protein and healthy fats. The first time I made it, we polished off the jar in one day and now it's a staple none of us can live without. The kids snack on it, I add it to smoothies or açai bowls, and my husband loves it the old-fashioned way—with coconut yogurt and fruit. The best part is that it's now a breakfast item I feel great about offering any day of the week.

MAKES 4 CUPS

½ cup raw **pumpkin seeds**

½ cup **walnut pieces**

½ cup **whole unsalted almonds**

½ cup **Brazil nuts**

¼ cup **hazelnuts**

¼ cup **shredded unsweetened coconut**

¼ cup **coconut oil**, melted

¼ cup **pure maple syrup**

2 teaspoons **pure vanilla extract**

Fine sea salt

1. Preheat the oven to 375°F. Line a baking sheet with parchment paper.
2. In a food processor, pulse together the pumpkin seeds, walnuts, almonds, Brazil nuts, hazelnuts, shredded coconut, coconut oil, maple syrup, vanilla, and a pinch of the salt. The mixture should resemble a coarsely chopped nut mixture in which each of the pieces is about the size of a lentil.
3. Dump the nut mixture onto the prepared baking sheet in a single compact layer, creating the look of a flat dough.
4. Bake for 15 to 20 minutes, until the nuts are fragrant and the mixture is lightly browned and dry. Remove from the oven and allow to cool for 15 minutes. Transfer the baking sheet to the refrigerator and cool for 10 minutes more.
5. Break the granola into desired-size pieces and store in an airtight container at room temperature for up to 2 weeks.

Morning Glory Açai Bowl

WITH HOMEMADE GRANOLA AND TAHINI HONEY DRIZZLE

Açai bowls are my favorite food group. I could happily eat one daily for breakfast, even in the winter, and sometimes I do. I choose unsweetened açai and rely on frozen bananas and blueberries for sweetness and extra antioxidants. Getting the perfect ratio of liquid to frozen açai/fruit is important. Remember: Less is more if you want that perfect thick and creamy consistency that we all lust over on Instagram. Start with the liquid specified in the recipe; you can always add a little more if you want it to be more smoothie-like, and sometimes I do this during colder months. You really can go wild with your toppings; I typically serve them with fresh fruit, homemade Power Protein Granola, and a drizzle of tahini, and then I feel great about all of us eating these bowls for breakfast because I know they are protein-packed and nutrient-dense as well as delicious.

SERVES 2

1 frozen peeled **banana**

1 (3.5-ounce) pouch frozen unsweetened **açai**

½ cup frozen **wild blueberries**

3 to 4 tablespoons unsweetened **coconut water**

For Serving

1 ripe **banana**, peeled

4 **strawberries**, hulled

½ cup **fresh blueberries**

½ cup **Power Protein Granola** (page 84)

2 tablespoons unsweetened **coconut flakes**

2 tablespoons **honey**

2 tablespoons **tahini**

1. In a high-speed blender or food processor, combine the frozen banana, açai, and frozen blueberries. Blend, adding 1 tablespoon of the coconut water at a time until the desired consistency is achieved, stopping as needed to scrape the sides of the blender with a rubber spatula. (If your blender has a tamper, you can also use this throughout the blending process.)

2. Divide the açai mixture between 2 bowls. Slice the ripe banana and the strawberries and evenly divide them between the bowls. Divide the fresh blueberries between the bowls, adding ¼ cup to each. Finish by adding ¼ cup of the granola, 1 tablespoon of the coconut flakes, 1 tablespoon of the honey, and 1 tablespoon of the tahini to each of the bowls. Serve immediately, while cold.

Hippie Dippy Scrambled Tofu

It doesn't get more old-school hippie vegetarian breakfast than scrambled tofu, but it doesn't get more delicious either. This is my favorite savory breakfast to make on the fly, and the kids love it too. This is a humble version that relies on the quick caramelized onion and pepper and vibrant curry powder, paprika, and a hit of tamari, but you can jazz it up with any veggies in your fridge. Sometimes I throw in a bunch of chopped-up leftovers from dinner the night before like sautéed string beans or roasted potatoes. Slice some avocado on top and add a hit of hot sauce. Whichever way you scramble it, it hits the spot.

SERVES 4 TO 6

4 tablespoons **avocado oil**

1 large **white onion**, chopped

1 large **red bell pepper**, chopped

Fine sea salt

1 (14-ounce) package **extra-firm tofu**, drained and patted dry with a paper towel

1 tablespoon **sweet paprika**

1 tablespoon mild **curry powder**

3 tablespoons **low-sodium tamari**

1 cup chopped **baby spinach**

Diced avocado, hot sauce, and/or **sesame seeds**, for garnish

1. In a large skillet, heat 2 tablespoons of the avocado oil over medium-high heat. Once glistening, add the onion, pepper, and a heavy pinch of salt. Sauté until the pepper becomes soft and the onion is translucent, about 5 minutes.

2. While the vegetables cook, crumble the tofu onto a plate, continuing to pat dry as needed.

3. When the onion begins to caramelize, add the paprika, curry powder, and another pinch of salt. Stir to combine. Remove the onion and pepper from the pan and place in a small bowl.

4. In the same pan, add the remaining 2 tablespoons avocado oil. Add the crumbled tofu, breaking it up with the back of a wooden spoon. The mixture should resemble scrambled eggs.

5. Spread the mixture in a single layer and cook undisturbed for 3 to 4 minutes, until the bottom of the layer is browned. Stir the tofu mixture and then leave it undisturbed to cook and brown for 2 to 3 minutes more. Continue this process until the tofu is browned throughout.

6. Reduce the heat to medium and stir in the tamari and spinach. Return the cooked onion mixture to the pan, stirring until fully combined and the spinach is completely wilted. Taste for seasoning.

7. Serve immediately, garnished with the avocado, hot sauce, and/or sesame seeds.

The Tutti-Frutti Chopped

I can't think about my childhood without this fruit salad coming to mind. My mom usually made it first thing in the morning for breakfast or for an after-school snack. I promise it's worth the bit of extra effort it takes to dice all the fruit, and sticking with mostly seasonal options will maximize sweetness. The stars of the show are the freshly squeezed orange juice, raisins, and shredded coconut that bring this from your average fruit salad to a recipe worthy of being in this book. It looks and tastes like a bowl of candy. I love to make this for our family or put it out for brunch when guests come over, and it always steals the show. When my kids have a sweet tooth, I will happily make this for them, and usually it hits the spot. If you want to make it extra sweet and decadent, add chopped dates.

SERVES 4 TO 6

2 medium **Anjou pears**

1 **banana**, peeled

1 medium **Granny Smith apple**

8 medium to large **strawberries**, hulled

1 cup **blueberries**

2 **oranges**

1 cup **raisins**

1 cup unsweetened **shredded coconut**

1. Dice the pears, banana, apple, and strawberries into ¼-inch pieces and place in a large bowl. Add the blueberries.

2. Remove the top and bottom of each orange and place it on one of its flat surfaces. Using your knife, cut between the peel and flesh, working around the orange to remove the peel. Supreme the oranges by cutting on either side of each segment to release the fruit from the membrane. Place the orange segments in the bowl with the other fruit and reserve the skeleton of the oranges.

3. Add the raisins and shredded coconut to the bowl, and with a large spoon, toss the mixture together. Juice the remains of the oranges over the entire mixture and toss again. (This salad is best served immediately but can be made up to 2 days in advance and stored, covered, in the refrigerator.)

Smashed Chickpea Frittata

I love to find savory and satiating breakfast items that don't involve eggs. My eldest son hates eggs, and I run hot and cold on them, so I've had to get creative with beautiful and hearty breakfast options. This one doesn't disappoint. Frittatas are wonderful because you can prepare them in one pan and get loads of veggies in. Here the chickpeas are smashed and take the place of eggs, the shallots and sun-dried tomatoes give a rich umami flavor, and the spinach brightens the whole thing. You can use your favorite jar of tomato sauce, and feel free to omit the feta if you don't eat dairy (but if you do eat dairy, this is one of those instances where the cheese really takes the dish up a notch). If you want to serve this when entertaining, it can easily be made a few hours before and then heated up when your guests arrive, but it is also delicious served at room temperature and enjoyed with some toasted and buttered sourdough.

SERVES 4 TO 6

2 tablespoons **avocado oil**

2 or 3 small **shallots**, chopped

½ **white onion**, chopped

8 **sun-dried tomatoes** packed in oil, chopped

2 cups chopped **spinach**

2 (13-ounce) jars **chickpeas**, such as Jovial, or 2 (15-ounce) cans, rinsed and drained

1 cup **tomato sauce**, such as Rao's Marinara

1 cup crumbled **sheep's-milk feta cheese**

Extra-virgin olive oil, for garnish (optional)

1. Preheat the oven to 375°F.
2. In a large nonstick ovenproof skillet, heat the avocado oil over medium heat. Add the shallots, onion, and sun-dried tomatoes to the skillet and cook, stirring occasionally, until the shallots and onion are translucent, 2 to 3 minutes.
3. Stir in the spinach and cook until the spinach is wilted and fully incorporated into the vegetable mixture, about 1 minute.
4. Add the chickpeas to a large bowl. Using a potato masher, fork, or your hands, mash the chickpeas until they're almost fully smashed, revealing their slightly tacky and potato-like filling consistently throughout the mixture.
5. Add the chickpeas to the skillet and, using a wooden spoon, stir them into the vegetable mixture. Create one even layer, flattening the mixture, and cook, undisturbed, for 4 to 5 minutes. Top with the tomato sauce and feta, then place the skillet in the oven and bake for 10 minutes.
6. Remove the skillet from the oven and cool the frittata slightly. Drizzle with the extra-virgin olive oil as a garnish, if desired. Serve hot, room temperature, or cold. (The frittata will keep in an airtight container in the refrigerator for up to 2 days.)

The Superhero Burrito

(WITH TOFU OR EGG)

Years ago, when I opened Spring Café in Aspen, I told our wonderful chef Blanca that I wanted to create the perfect breakfast burrito that was satiating but also healthy and left you feeling full but light before a day of skiing. I showed her some inspiration, and we tested many a recipe. One morning I walked into the café, and she had a burrito waiting for me. I took a bite and knew we'd created the most delicious vegetarian breakfast burrito. I named it the Superhero Burrito, and we put it on our menu that day. By the weekend it was a bestseller, and eleven years later it remains our top-selling item in both Aspen and New York. If you've visited our cafés and you're a Superhero devotee, I hope this inspires you to make it at home and put your own spin on it.

MAKES 4 BURRITOS

2 tablespoons **avocado oil**

1 small **yellow onion**, diced

2 **Yukon Gold potatoes**, diced

1 **red bell pepper**, diced

1 **green bell pepper**, diced

1 (8-ounce) package **cremini or button mushrooms**, coarsely chopped

2 teaspoons **fine sea salt**, or more to taste

2 teaspoons **ground turmeric**

2 teaspoons mild **curry powder**

2 teaspoons **ground cumin**

1 (14-ounce) package **extra-firm tofu**, cubed, drained, and with a paper towel, or 6 or 7 large eggs, beaten

1 cup grated **vegan cheese**

4 gluten-free burrito-size **tortillas** or 8 gluten-free small tortillas, such as Siete Foods

1. In a large skillet, heat the avocado oil over medium heat. Add the onion, potatoes, red pepper, green pepper, and mushrooms. Season the vegetables with 1 teaspoon of the salt and cook for 5 to 7 minutes, stirring occasionally with a wooden spoon, until the vegetables are reduced in size and tender and the onion is translucent.

2. Add the turmeric, curry powder, and cumin and fully incorporate them into the vegetable mixture. Cook for an additional 5 minutes to toast the spices. Add a few tablespoons of water to the pan to release any spices or brown bits from the bottom of the pan.

3. If using tofu, add it to the pan, tossing with the seasoned vegetables. Some of the tofu cubes may break or crumble slightly. Season with ½ teaspoon salt, tasting and modifying the seasoning. If using eggs, add them to the pan and, using a spatula, continuously combine the eggs and vegetables while the eggs cook. Season with the remaining ½ teaspoon salt. Cook until the eggs are firm, about 2 minutes. Stir in the cheese and cook until the cheese has melted, about 1 minute more.

4. To assemble the burrito, warm each tortilla over the stovetop using direct heat (if you have an electric range) or in a large skillet (if you have a gas range). Add 2 cups of the filling to the center of each of the large burrito tortillas or 1 cup to the center of each of the small tortillas. Fold the bottom of the burrito over the filling and gently pull it back toward you, encasing the filling. Fold up the right and left sides and then roll upward, creating a cylinder. Cut in half, seam-side down, and serve.

5. If not rolling immediately, the burrito filling can be stored in an airtight container in the refrigerator for up to 3 days.

Diner-Style Home Fries

You may be sensing a theme; I love an old-school diner-style breakfast. The irony isn't lost on me. Diners aren't exactly known for their organic eggs and seed-oil-free dishes, so let me explain. I grew up in a small town, and for all the mom-made, healthy, organic breakfasts that fueled my childhood, there were also some early-morning trips to the local breakfast joint with my dad before my mom woke up. I appreciate a greasy, perfectly cooked home-fry as much as the next gal, but these days I prefer them cooked in nonrancid avocado oil, so I created this recipe. The trick is using an obscene amount of paprika and throwing in a finely diced bell pepper and onion, which naturally caramelize as the potatoes roast, adding a perfect bit of sweetness.

SERVES 6 TO 8

1 large **onion**, diced

1 **orange bell pepper**, diced

9 **Yukon Gold potatoes**, diced

¼ cup **avocado oil**

2 teaspoons **smoked paprika**

1 teaspoon **garlic powder**

1 teaspoon **fine sea salt**

Freshly ground **black pepper**

1. Preheat the oven to 375°F. Line a baking sheet with parchment paper.
2. In a large bowl, combine the onion, bell pepper, potatoes, avocado oil, paprika, garlic powder, salt, and black pepper to taste. Using a rubber spatula, toss to thoroughly coat the potatoes. Spread evenly in a single layer on the prepared baking sheet.
3. Add 2 tablespoons water to the baking sheet. Roast for 40 to 45 minutes, flipping the potatoes and rotating the baking sheet halfway, until the potatoes are tender and slightly browned.
4. Remove the home fries from the oven and allow them to cool slightly before serving. These can be served hot, warm, or at room temperature.

Light Bites

Green Herb Whipped Feta

WITH RAW HONEY AND CHILE FLAKES

This is a quick dip that always wows my guests when I'm entertaining. I love to serve it with pita, buttery toasted baguette, or gluten-free sourdough. When you process feta in a food processor, it develops a whipped consistency, which takes this briny cheese to a whole other level! I love the combination of sweet honey and tangy, salty cheese, and the chopped parsley and chile flakes balance it all out to give you a flavor bomb in every bite. You can change the toppings seasonally, mixing and matching herbs and spices to your taste.

MAKES ABOUT 2 CUPS

1 (1-pound) block **sheep's-milk feta cheese**, drained if in liquid

Gluten-free pita

1 teaspoon **red pepper flakes**

1 tablespoon **extra-virgin olive oil**

1 tablespoon **raw honey**

Crudités, for serving

¼ cup chopped **fresh flat-leaf parsley**

1. In a food processor, process the feta until smooth and creamy.

2. Slice pita into wedges, toast until just crispy and drizzle with olive oil.

3. Place the whipped feta cheese into a serving bowl and top with the parsley and red pepper flakes. Drizzle the olive oil and honey decoratively on top and serve immediately with crudités and pita bread, or store in an airtight container in the refrigerator for up to 3 days.

Simple Hippie Hummus

WITH CRUNCHY VEGGIES AND TAHINI DRIZZLE

Everybody has an opinion on how to make the best and creamiest hummus. I'm not going to pretend that I am a hummus expert, but I am deeply and fanatically in love with this hummus. This is not the super fluffy and extra tahini-rich kind you would find at a Middle Eastern restaurant, though I do love that as well. This is more the hummus you find in health food stores and restaurants, and it's like the one my mom made me when I was a kid. I subscribe to two universal truths when making hummus: The best hummus comes from warm, freshly pressure-cooked chickpeas, and from slowly drizzling ice water into the food processor while blending them. That's how you get the smoothest consistency. You can absolutely use jarred or canned beans, however. Just warm them up before blending, and you will still have a delicious hummus.

MAKES ABOUT 2 CUPS

1½ cups **cooked chickpeas**, or 1 (13-ounce) jar chickpeas, such as Jovial, or 1 (15-ounce) can, drained and rinsed

Juice of 1 **lemon**

2 tablespoons **tahini**, plus more to garnish

1 tablespoon **extra-virgin olive oil**, plus more to garnish

½ teaspoon **fine sea salt**

2 to 4 tablespoons **ice water**

Assorted crudités, for serving

1. In a food processor, process the chickpeas, lemon juice, tahini, olive oil, and salt until just combined. With the machine running, slowly add up to 4 tablespoons of the ice water, 1 tablespoon at a time, and blend until the hummus is smooth and creamy.

2. Place the hummus in a serving dish and garnish with an additional drizzle of tahini and olive oil. Serve with crudités. If not eating immediately, store in an airtight container in the refrigerator for up to 3 days.

Feel-Good Nachos

I could eat nachos weekly, if not daily, and thanks to this recipe I do. If you're sensitive to corn, you can use a cassava-based tortilla chip, but whatever chip you use, think of them as a vehicle to load on lots of great, healthy ingredients. The trick to delicious nachos is to bake the chips with just the beans and cheese, and then add all the toppings. This will ensure you have extra-crispy and not soggy nachos. I stick with the classic combination of black beans and cheese and then, once they're cooked, load them with lettuce, guacamole, pico de gallo, and any other chopped veggies I have laying around. My kids beg for these nachos, and I always feel good about making them. Turns out my kids will eat almost anything if it's sitting atop a crunchy, cheesy baked chip.

SERVES 4 TO 6

1 pound **tortilla chips**

1 (15-ounce) can **black beans,** drained and rinsed

1 pound **vegan cheese or goat cheese,** shredded or crumbled

1 tablespoon **avocado oil**

2 cups **guacamole,** homemade (see page 39) or store-bought

1 cup **pico de gallo,** homemade (see page 40) or store-bought

1 head **romaine lettuce,** thinly sliced

½ cup **plant-based sour cream,** for garnish

1. Preheat the oven to 375°F.

2. On a large baking sheet, lay the tortilla chips in a single layer. Evenly distribute the beans and cheese over the chips and drizzle with the avocado oil. Bake for 10 minutes, or until the cheese is melted and bubbly.

3. Top the nachos with the guacamole, dolloping in a few areas, and then evenly scatter the pico and lettuce on top.

4. In a small bowl, thin out the sour cream with about 1 tablespoon of water, or until the consistency of maple syrup is achieved. Drizzle the sour cream over the nachos and serve immediately.

Lemony White Bean Dip

WITH TOASTED PITA

This bean dip is an excellent source of plant protein and works as an afternoon snack for the kids or as a beautiful appetizer for entertaining. White beans are less starchy than chickpeas, so this dip is thinner than traditional hummus but still very satisfying. The lemon, garlic, and parsley keep it fresh and light. I make my own pita chips by slicing gluten-free pita into triangles and toasting them until crispy. If you're making this for a dinner party, you could also serve it with some radishes and carrots, which look vibrant against the white dip.

MAKES ABOUT 2 CUPS

1 (13-ounce) jar **white beans**, such as Jovial, or 1 (15-ounce) can

Juice of 2 **lemons**

1 tablespoon **extra-virgin olive oil**, plus more to garnish

½ teaspoon **fine sea salt**

1 to 3 tablespoons **ice water**

2 tablespoons chopped **flat-leaf parsley**, for garnish

Toasted **gluten-free pita chips or crackers**, for serving

Assorted crudités, for serving (optional)

1. In a food processor, process the white beans, lemon juice, olive oil, and salt until just combined. With the machine running, slowly add up to 3 tablespoons of the ice water, 1 tablespoon at a time, and continue to process until the dip is smooth. (This dip will be thinner than the hummus on page 102.)

2. Pour the dip into a serving dish and garnish with the parsley and an additional drizzle of olive oil. Serve with toasted pita chips or crackers and/or crudités.

Buttery Pecans

WITH CRISPY SAGE

This recipe was a happy accident: I was toasting pecans for a kale salad and decided to crisp up some fresh sage in the same pan at the last moment. I placed the pecans and sage in a bowl while I finished preparing the salad and by the time I was ready to mix them in I had devoured them. That's when I realized these nuts were good enough to have their own recipe! Place them with crudités on cheese boards, serve them at dinner parties, or make mason jars full and give them as gifts during the holidays. They are buttery and salty and just perfect!

MAKES 2 CUPS

4 tablespoons (½ stick) **unsalted butter**

5 or 6 **fresh sage leaves**

2 cups **pecans**

½ teaspoon **fine sea salt**

½ teaspoon **garlic powder**

½ teaspoon **onion powder**

Maldon **flaky sea salt**

1. In a large skillet, melt 2 tablespoons of the butter over medium heat. When the butter is melted, add the sage leaves and cook for 1 to 2 minutes per side. The leaves will bubble and darken slightly but they should not brown. Transfer the leaves to a plate lined with a paper towel and allow them to cool completely.

2. Wipe the skillet clean and melt the remaining 2 tablespoons butter over medium heat. Add the pecans and toast for 3 to 5 minutes, or until the nuts are fragrant and slightly toasted. Remove the skillet from the heat and transfer the pecans to a medium bowl. Stir in the fine sea salt, garlic powder, and onion powder.

3. Using your hands, tear or crush the sage leaves (they will be slightly crispy) into the pecan mixture and stir to combine. Finish with a sprinkle of flaky sea salt. Serve immediately or allow them to cool completely and store in an airtight container at room temperature for up to 1 week.

Dinner Party Antipasti Board

My parents always preferred to entertain at home rather than go out to dinner. They usually invited friends over on Friday or Saturday nights, and my mom would always set out a big board of "nosh" when guests arrived. She had a porcelain platter painted with olives and wisteria vines, and on it she would arrange roasted red peppers and eggplant dip, marinated olives, raw goat cheese, and fresh sourdough from the local bakery. She'd always include her homemade white bean dip and tons of colorful crudités. There were little bowls of nuts and fig jam, and a good olive oil for dipping. My mouth still waters when I think about her platter, and I try to re-create it whenever we invite friends over for dinner. I've perfected some of my own staples over the years, like this Baked Goat Brie with honey and sage, and the addictive Savory Sesame Cashews. Of course, you can add any of your favorite dips or snacks, and even substitute store-bought for homemade if you're pressed for time. The point of a party board is to bring people together and share healthy, beautiful food, and my mom honored that more than anyone.

SERVES 4 TO 6

1 pint (16 ounces) assorted pitted marinated **olives**

1 bunch **radishes**, leafy tops and roots trimmed

3 heads **endive**, leaves separated

Baked Goat Brie (recipe follows)

Roasted Red Peppers (recipe follows)

Savory Sesame Cashews (recipe follows)

Roasted Garlic White Beans (recipe follows)

Gluten-free or seeded **crackers**

½ (16-ounce) block **sheep's-milk feta cheese**, drained if in liquid

Place the olives in a small bowl and situate it on a large platter or cutting board. Scatter the radishes and endive spears around the platter. Add the Brie and a small knife for serving to the platter. Place the roasted red peppers, sesame cashews, garlic white beans, crackers, and feta block in small individual bowls or alongside the Brie, with small forks or other utensils for serving.

Recipe continues

BAKED GOAT BRIE

SERVES 4 TO 6

1 (8-ounce) wheel goat Brie cheese

4 or 5 large fresh sage leaves

2 teaspoons raw honey

1 teaspoon extra-virgin olive oil

½ teaspoon dried oregano

½ teaspoon dried thyme

½ teaspoon dried rosemary

¼ teaspoon Maldon flaky sea salt

1. Preheat the oven to 350°F.

2. Slice the wheel of Brie horizontally. Shingle sage leaves on the cut side of the Brie wheel and drizzle with 1 teaspoon of the honey. Sandwich the Brie wheel back together and place in a baking dish. Drizzle the Brie with the remaining teaspoon of honey and the olive oil. Sprinkle the oregano, thyme, rosemary, and flaky sea salt on top.

3. Bake the Brie wheel for about 15 minutes, or until soft and slightly browned. Serve immediately.

ROASTED RED PEPPERS

MAKES 1 CUP

3 red bell peppers

2 tablespoons extra-virgin olive oil

½ teaspoon fine sea salt

1. Place a rack in the middle of the oven and preheat the broiler to high.

2. Place the peppers on a baking sheet and drizzle with the olive oil. Sprinkle the peppers with ¼ teaspoon of the salt and place the baking sheet on the rack. Using tongs, rotate the peppers occasionally, until they are blackened and charred on all sides. Depending on the strength of the broiler, this can take anywhere from 5 to 15 minutes.

3. Remove the peppers from the oven and place in a large glass bowl. Cover the bowl with plastic wrap and allow the peppers to steam for 5 to 10 minutes to help loosen the skins.

4. Using a paper towel, remove and discard the peppers' tops, skins, and seeds. Cut the peppers into ½-inch-wide strips, and season with the remaining ¼ teaspoon salt.

5. Serve immediately, or store in an airtight container in the refrigerator for up to 1 week.

ROASTED GARLIC WHITE BEANS

MAKES ABOUT 2 CUPS

1 garlic head

¼ cup plus 1 tablespoon extra-virgin olive oil

½ teaspoon fine sea salt

1 (13-ounce) jar white beans, such as Jovial, or 1 (15-ounce) can, drained and rinsed

3 or 4 herb sprigs, such as thyme or rosemary

1. Preheat the oven to 350°F.

2. Remove ¼ inch of the top of the garlic head, exposing the cloves.

3. Place the head of garlic on a piece of parchment paper and season with 1 tablespoon of the olive oil and ¼ teaspoon of the salt. Fold the parchment over the garlic and seal the edges tight to create a packet. Place the package on a baking sheet and roast for 45 to 60 minutes. The garlic is done when it is golden, caramelized, and tender.

4. Remove the roasted garlic from the oven and carefully open the parchment package. Cool for at least 5 minutes and then gently squeeze the garlic cloves out of their papery skins and into a medium bowl. To the bowl, add the remaining ¼ cup olive oil, ¼ teaspoon salt, the beans, and fresh herbs and toss.

5. Serve immediately, or store in an airtight container in the refrigerator for up 1 week.

SAVORY SESAME CASHEWS

MAKES 3 CUPS

2 cups cashews

¼ cup sesame seeds

1 tablespoon avocado oil

1 tablespoon raw honey

1 teaspoon sweet paprika

1 teaspoon onion powder

½ teaspoon fine sea salt

½ teaspoon red pepper flakes

Freshly cracked black pepper

1. Preheat the oven to 325°F. Line a baking sheet with parchment paper.

2. In a large bowl, combine the cashews, sesame seeds, avocado oil, honey, paprika, onion powder, salt, red pepper flakes, and black pepper. Toss to fully combine and then spread them in a single layer on the baking sheet. Roast for 20 to 25 minutes, or until the nuts are golden brown and fragrant. Remove from the oven and cool completely before breaking into clumps.

3. Serve immediately, or store in an airtight container at room temperature for up to 2 weeks.

Salads

Kitchen Sink Chopped Salad

This is the salad I make when I want to use up every vegetable in my refrigerator. The fine chop ensures that even veggie-discerning family members or guests will dig in. Even a self-professed zucchini hater like my middle child doesn't complain about the small pieces of crunchy raw zucchini coated in a delicious lemony-Dijon dressing. I love this salad so much that I wind up spearing forkfuls into my mouth straight from the mixing bowl and finishing it before I've even had a chance to properly toss and serve it. I've given you a blueprint here based on what I usually have on hand, but the beauty of this salad is that it can be made from whatever you have around at any given moment. This salad is hearty enough to be a meal, especially if you want to add extra fat or protein like sliced avocado or grilled tempeh. I'm very openly not a batch cooker or meal planner, but if you are, you can make a big batch of this salad, keep the dressing on the side, and eat it for three days. If that gets you to pack more plants into your diet, then I wholeheartedly recommend it.

SERVES 4 TO 6

3 **radishes**

3 **celery stalks**

3 medium **carrots**

2 medium **cucumbers**

2 small **zucchini**

2 **red bell peppers**

1 head **romaine lettuce**

¼ head **green cabbage**

½ cup chopped pitted **green olives**, such as Castelvetrano

½ cup **extra-virgin olive oil**

Juice of 1 **lemon**

½ teaspoon **fine sea salt**

1 teaspoon **Dijon mustard**

1 **garlic clove**, peeled

1 **avocado**, diced

1. Chop or dice the radishes, celery, carrots, cucumbers, zucchini, peppers, romaine, and cabbage into ½-inch or ¼-inch cubes, depending on your preference and the quality of your knife skills. The key is to be consistent so that each piece is the same size. Place all the vegetables in a large bowl with the olives.

2. In a small bowl, whisk together the olive oil, lemon juice, salt, Dijon mustard, and 1 teaspoon water. Using a Microplane, grate the garlic into the bowl and mix to combine.

3. Before serving, add the diced avocado to the salad, add the desired amount of dressing, and toss to combine. Extra dressing can be stored in an airtight container in the refrigerator for up to 1 week.

Greek 'n' Greens

If there's one salad that I could eat on repeat for the rest of my life it's a Greek salad, and whenever I'm hungry and in a hurry to make something, it's my go-to. Traditionally, Greek salads don't have lettuce, but I am a lettuce girl. One day I was frantically chopping cucumbers, tomatoes, and peppers before school pickup, and I was too rushed and lazy to chop lettuce so I took a romaine heart, sliced it in half, and dumped the Greek salad on top, then added extra dressing. I didn't even use a knife and fork—I just picked up the entire romaine boat like you would a sandwich. As I ate it, I realized it was the most genius way to add lettuce to a Greek salad. Now I make a slightly more refined version when I have guests coming over or when I serve this for dinner (as I frequently do)—but fork and knife remain optional.

SERVES 4 TO 6

3 heads **romaine lettuce**, halved lengthwise

3 large **beefsteak tomatoes**, diced

3 small **Persian cucumbers** or 1 **English cucumber**, diced

3 **red bell peppers**, diced

1 cup pitted **kalamata olives**

½ cup and 1 tablespoon **extra-virgin olive oil**

¼ cup **red wine vinegar**

2 tablespoons **dried oregano**

Juice of 1 **lemon**

½ teaspoon **fine sea salt**

1 (1-pound) block **sheep's-milk feta cheese**, drained if in liquid

1. Lay the romaine halves cut-side up on a large platter. Scatter the diced tomatoes, cucumbers, bell peppers, and olives on the romaine.

2. In a small bowl, whisk together ½ cup of the olive oil, the red wine vinegar, 1 tablespoon of the oregano, the lemon juice, and salt until fully emulsified. Pour the desired amount of the dressing over the decorated romaine.

3. Evenly cut the block of feta into 6 squares or triangles and sprinkle them evenly with the remaining 1 tablespoon oregano. Top each romaine half with a piece of the oregano-dusted feta and drizzle with the remaining 1 tablespoon olive oil. Extra dressing can be stored in an airtight container in the refrigerator for up to 1 week.

Big Italian Delicatessen Salad

I went to elementary and middle school near a health food store named Fresh Fields, which was later acquired by Whole Foods. Fresh Fields had an antipasti bar that was out-of-this-world delicious. My mom used to take me there most days after pickup, and we'd make a container of all the different selections. Herby olives, roasted artichoke hearts soaked in olive oil, marinated red peppers, and button mushrooms were some of the standouts. While my mom shopped, I ate, savoring every vinegary bite, olive oil dripping down my chin. This salad is my homage to those after-school grocery shopping trips. I throw in hearts of palm and white beans for added protein, since I often make this for lunch. There's no lettuce or tender veggies in this mix, which means it's a great make-ahead salad. You could even put a small bowl on the Dinner Party Antipasti Board (page 110) when you are entertaining.

SERVES 4 TO 6

1 (13-ounce) jar **white beans**, such as Jovial, or 1 (15-ounce) can, drained and rinsed

2 **roasted red peppers**, chopped

2 cups chopped **hearts of palm**

1 cup pitted **green olives**, such as Castelvetrano, chopped

1 cup chopped **artichoke hearts**

1 cup **banana peppers**, sliced

¼ cup chopped **fresh flat-leaf parsley**

¼ cup **extra-virgin olive oil**

Juice of 1 **lemon**

Maldon **flaky sea salt** (optional)

1. In a large bowl, combine the beans, roasted red peppers, hearts of palm, olives, artichoke hearts, banana peppers, and parsley. Toss until fully combined.

2. Dress the salad with the olive oil and lemon juice and toss again to fully distribute the dressing. Season with flaky sea salt, if needed. Serve immediately or store in an airtight container in the refrigerator for up to 1 week.

The Vegetarian Niçoise

A Niçoise salad has everything I love most in the vegetable kingdom: delicate butter lettuce, small waxy potatoes, radishes, and olives. I would order a Niçoise every time I see it on a menu, save for the tuna, which I don't eat. This version is with chickpeas in place of tuna, and it's my favorite way to prepare a vegetarian Niçoise. If you want to mimic the texture and flavor of tinned fish, the sun-dried-tomato oil and caper brine really do the trick here, so make sure to use them when mashing your chickpeas. For the final flavor element, I dress this salad with my If You Love Mustard Vinaigrette.

SERVES 4 TO 6

8 small **red new potatoes** (about 2 pounds total)

1 pound **string beans**, trimmed

1 head **butter lettuce**, leaves separated

1 (13-ounce) jar **chickpeas**, such as Jovial, or 1 (15-ounce) can, rinsed and drained

3 tablespoons **capers**, with brine

5 oil-packed **sun-dried tomatoes**

⅛ teaspoon **fine sea salt**

1 pint **cherry tomatoes**, halved

10 to 12 **radishes**, halved

1 cup pitted **kalamata olives**

4 **Hard-Boiled Eggs**, halved lengthwise

If You Love Mustard Vinaigrette (page 33)

1. In a medium saucepan, cover the potatoes with cold water. Bring to a boil over medium-high heat, then reduce to a simmer. Cook the potatoes until fork-tender, 12 to 15 minutes. Drain them and, when cool enough to handle, slice them in half.

2. Refill the saucepan with water and bring to a boil over medium-high heat. Blanch the string beans until bright green, about 2 minutes. Drain the string beans in a colander and immediately run under cold water, or place in an ice bath, to stop the cooking.

3. Meanwhile, line a large serving platter with the butter lettuce.

4. In a medium bowl, combine the chickpeas, 2 tablespoons of the capers with their brine, the sun-dried tomatoes, and salt. Using a fork, mash the mixture together until the ingredients are broken down and resemble the consistency of tuna fish. Place the chickpea mixture on the platter.

5. Add the potatoes and string beans to the platter, arranging so that each has its own area of the plate. Similarly, arrange the cherry tomatoes, radishes, olives, and eggs on the platter. Scatter the remaining 1 tablespoon capers over everything and drizzle the vinaigrette on top.

6. Serve immediately, or cover and store in the refrigerator for up to 2 hours before serving.

Warm Kale Salad

WITH ROASTED SWEET POTATOES AND QUINOA

I am a year-round salad-a-day gal, but come the dead of winter my body and taste buds start craving warm food, especially for lunch, which is when I typically eat my largest salad. Kale is always my go-to green for this type of winter salad, because the firm leaves hold up so well under a pile of warm grains and hearty sweet potatoes. Quinoa is naturally gluten-free and is an excellent source of plant protein because it contains all nine essential amino acids. While it sometimes gets a bad rap for being "bland," if you know how to cook it, the nutty, fluffy consistency rivals even the best rice. I add a little ginger here to liven up the grains and balance out the slightly sweet maple-Dijon vinaigrette.

SERVES 4 TO 6

2 large **sweet potatoes**, peeled and chopped

¼ cup **avocado oil**

¼ teaspoon **fine sea salt**

¼ teaspoon **garlic powder**

¼ teaspoon **onion powder**

⅛ teaspoon **ground nutmeg**

Freshly **cracked black pepper**

1 cup **quinoa**

1 **garlic clove**, peeled

1 (1-inch) piece **fresh ginger**, peeled

½ cup **extra-virgin olive oil**

¼ cup **balsamic vinegar**

2 tablespoons **Dijon mustard**

Juice of 1 **lemon**

2 teaspoons **pure maple syrup**

2 heads **curly kale**, stems removed and leaves torn (about 10 cups)

1. Preheat the oven to 425°F.

2. Place the sweet potatoes on a baking sheet. Drizzle with the avocado oil and season with ⅛ teaspoon of the salt, the garlic powder, onion powder, nutmeg, and black pepper. Using your hands or a spoon, toss to fully coat the potatoes and then arrange in a single layer. Roast for 30 to 35 minutes, until the potatoes are tender and golden brown. Remove from the oven and allow them to cool slightly.

3. While the sweet potatoes are roasting, combine the quinoa and 2 cups water in a medium saucepan. (If using presoaked quinoa, reduce the water to 1½ cups.) Grate the garlic and ginger into the saucepan and bring to a boil over medium-high heat. When the mixture reaches a boil, reduce the heat to low and cover the pot. Continue to cook the quinoa for 12 to 14 minutes, until all the water has evaporated and the quinoa is tender and sprouted. Remove the quinoa from the heat and allow the mixture to continue steaming, covered, for 10 minutes. After 10 minutes, remove the lid and fluff the quinoa with a fork.

4. In a small bowl, whisk together the olive oil, balsamic vinegar, mustard, lemon juice, maple syrup, the remaining ⅛ teaspoon salt, and some freshly cracked black pepper.

5. Place the kale in a large serving bowl. Add the warm sweet potatoes and quinoa and toss to wilt the greens slightly. Add the dressing and toss well to fully incorporate it into the salad.

6. Serve immediately, or store, covered, in the refrigerator until ready to serve. This salad will stand up to being dressed up to 2 hours ahead of time.

East Coast Cali-Mex Salad

This is a longtime fan favorite salad from Spring Café Aspen, inspired by the produce-forward Cali-Mex food I love to eat whenever I visit Los Angeles. Don't be dissuaded by the micro steps in the recipe; you can buy store-bought pico de gallo and tortilla chips and have yourself a delicious salad. But if you have a little time to make it all from scratch, it is well worth the effort. If you've ever made a taco salad, then you know how satisfying it is to have the crunchy shell crumbled on top. But in this salad, it's the tangy lime and coriander dressing and the sweet caramelized roasted corn that really take it up a level from just being a taco in a bowl. When I make it at home, I like to set out the components and let everyone assemble their own salad. But fully assembled and dressed, it's a showstopper, if you prefer to go that route.

SERVES 4 TO 6

1 to 2 tablespoons **avocado oil**

4 small **corn tortillas**, sliced into thin strips

¼ teaspoon **fine sea salt**

4 ears **corn**, shucked

3 heads **romaine lettuce**, diced

1 cup **pico de gallo**, homemade (see page 40) or store-bought

1½ cup **cooked black beans** or 1 (15-ounce) can black beans, drained and rinsed

1 cup drained **Pickled Onion** (recipe follows)

1 **garlic clove**, chopped

1 cup chopped **fresh cilantro**

½ cup fresh **lime juice**

1 tablespoon **agave nectar**

¼ teaspoon **ground coriander**

¾ teaspoon **fine sea salt**

Freshly **cracked black pepper**

1 cup **extra-virgin olive oil**

2 **avocados**

1. In a high-sided medium saucepan, heat the avocado oil over medium heat to 365°F. Working in batches, add the tortilla strips to the hot oil and cook until just toasted and crispy, 1 to 2 minutes. Use a slotted spoon to transfer the strips to a plate lined with paper towels and season with the salt.

2. Situate an oven rack about 6 inches away from the broiler. Preheat the broiler to high. Place the corn on a baking sheet and broil for 4 to 5 minutes per side, turning as needed, until the corn is evenly charred. Remove the corn and allow it to cool completely.

3. In a large bowl, combine the romaine, pico de gallo, beans, pickled onions, and tortilla strips.

4. In a small bowl, whisk together the garlic, cilantro, lime juice, agave, coriander, salt, and some pepper. While whisking, slowly stream in the olive oil until fully emulsified.

5. Dress the salad and toss to fully coat all the ingredients. When ready to serve, dice the avocados and gently toss into the salad to maintain individual avocado chunks.

PICKLED ONION

MAKES 1 QUART (ABOUT 1 CUP DRAINED PICKLED ONION)

¾ cup apple cider vinegar

1 teaspoon fine sea salt

¼ cup agave nectar

1 teaspoon whole black peppercorns

1 garlic clove, peeled

1 red onion, thinly sliced

In a medium saucepan, combine the apple cider vinegar, ¾ cup water, the salt, agave, peppercorns, and garlic clove. Bring to a simmer over medium heat. Place the onion in a large bowl. Once the liquid is simmering, pour it over the onion and allow the mixture to cool completely. When cooled, transfer the pickled onion with its liquid to an airtight container. The pickled onion can be stored in the container in the refrigerator for up to 1 month.

Shaved Fennel Salad

WITH LEMON, OLIVE OIL, AND JALAPEÑO

Fennel is an underrated vegetable. Most people never have it at the top of their grocery list, but in my opinion those people are seriously missing out, and this recipe is here to change that. I don't think anyone has anything against fennel, per se, but perhaps most people don't know what to do with it. Here it is thinly sliced, drenched in olive oil and tangy lemon, and dotted with chopped jalapeño for a little spice. The result is a crunchy, fresh, and perfect salad that I could literally eat by the bowlful for lunch or dinner. If I'm entertaining, I love to serve this with Pam's One and Only Vegetarian Lasagna (page 186), and I always make extra and throw a little on top of whatever bowl I'm making myself for lunch the next day. Fennel bulbs come in all shapes and sizes; for this recipe each bulb should give you about a cup of thinly sliced pieces. If you come up with less, just adjust the number of fennel bulbs in the recipe.

SERVES 6 TO 8

6 to 8 large **fennel bulbs**, thinly sliced, ¼ cup fronds reserved

1 teaspoon **fine sea salt**

1 **jalapeño**, seeded and minced

Juice of 2 **lemons**

¼ cup **extra-virgin olive oil**

1. Place the sliced fennel in a large bowl. Season the fennel with ½ teaspoon of the salt and, as you would a kale salad, massage the mixture slightly to soften the fennel. Add the jalapeño and stir to combine.

2. In a small bowl, whisk together the lemon juice and olive oil until emulsified. Season the dressing with the remaining ½ teaspoon salt.

3. Toss the salad with the reserved fennel fronds and the desired amount of dressing. Serve immediately.

Summer in a Bowl

This dish is one part recipe and three parts nostalgia. My dad's favorite food is ripe summer tomatoes. When I was a kid, he'd wait all year for tomato season, slice one open, top it with some goat cheese, and drizzle on copious amounts of olive oil and a dollop of mustard. I inherited his love for tomatoes and his method of eating them. I add a few chopped cucumbers and a little extra mustard; during peak tomato season, I can eat it daily. I love it for many reasons, but mostly because the first bite always takes me back to being poolside with my dad on a glorious August afternoon.

SERVES 4 TO 6

5 large **beefsteak tomatoes**, chopped

3 **English or Japanese cucumbers**, halved lengthwise, seeded, and sliced into ¼-inch-thick half-moons

¼ cup **extra-virgin olive oil**

2 tablespoons **Dijon mustard**

Maldon **flaky sea salt**

Place the tomatoes and cucumbers in a large bowl. Add the olive oil and mustard. Toss to combine and add flaky sea salt to taste.

Chicories

WITH BEETS, FENNEL, AND SEARED HALLOUMI

One of my favorite times of year at the farmers' market is late fall, when chicories abound. I can't get enough of the deep purple hues of Treviso radicchio and the purple and green varieties of endive. Because they are so beautiful, I always buy more than I need and often find myself with a refrigerator drawer filled with chicories that need to be used up—enter this salad. Halloumi becomes golden and tender when you sear it, and the sturdy radicchio leaves are a perfect vessel for scooping up salty bites of Halloumi and earthy beets. Chicories are best left whole or gently torn, so this is a salad I serve on a platter rather than in a bowl, with the light citrus vinaigrette drizzled on top.

SERVES 4 TO 6

4 or 5 medium **red beets**

1 head **radicchio**

3 heads **endive**

1 large **fennel bulb**

1 pound **Halloumi cheese**

Juice of ½ **orange**

¼ cup **extra-virgin olive oil**

2 tablespoons **apple cider vinegar**

¼ teaspoon **fine sea salt**

1. In a large pot, cover the beets with water and bring to a boil over medium-high heat. When the water reaches a boil, reduce the heat to medium and simmer until the beets are tender, 60 to 90 minutes, adding more water as needed to keep the beets submerged. Drain the beets and, once cool enough to handle, use paper towels to remove the skins and cut the beets into 1-inch pieces. (The peeled beets can be kept in an airtight container in the refrigerator for up to 3 days.)

2. While the beets are cooking, tear the radicchio and place on a large serving platter. Trim the bottoms off the endive, separate the leaves, and add them to the platter with the radicchio. Remove the bottom from the fennel and halve the bulbs lengthwise. Thinly slice the fennel and add the slices to the platter.

3. Slice the Halloumi into ¼-inch-thick slices. Heat a large skillet over medium heat. Add the Halloumi slices, working in batches as needed, and cook until the bottoms are golden brown, 1 to 2 minutes. Flip and cook the other side until golden brown, 1 to 2 minutes more. Remove the Halloumi from the pan and add to the platter with the chicories and fennel.

4. In a small bowl, whisk together the orange juice, olive oil, apple cider vinegar, and salt.

5. Add the beets to the salad and pour the salad dressing on top. Toss and serve immediately.

Little Gems

WITH OLIVES AND QUICK-MARINATED SHALLOTS

Little Gems need very little fuss to become a gorgeous salad. I make this when I don't have the time or energy to chop a bunch of lettuce greens or other vegetables but still want a crunchy and satisfying salad. Thanks to the marinated shallots, this salad is simple but not boring. I love it as a dinner salad because it's delicate and mild, but it's the perfect canvas if you want to add avocado or a hearty protein like white beans.

SERVES 4 TO 6

2 **shallots**, minced

2 tablespoons **apple cider vinegar**

Juice of ½ **lemon**

⅛ teaspoon **fine sea salt**

¼ cup **extra-virgin olive oil**

4 to 6 heads **Little Gem lettuce**, torn into bite-size pieces (10 to 12 cups total)

2 cups pitted **green olives**, such as Castelvetrano, chopped

1. In a medium bowl, combine the shallots, vinegar, lemon juice, and salt and allow the mixture to macerate for 5 minutes. Whisk in the olive oil, then cover and refrigerate the mixture for at least 30 minutes or up to 3 days.

2. In a large bowl, toss the lettuce, olives, and quick-marinated shallots to fully combine. Serve immediately.

Vegetables

Sesame Nori Broccoli

File this recipe under "one of the million ways I try to get my kids to eat broccoli." I stumbled upon this concoction by chance when my older boys were on a green-vegetable strike but would seemingly eat anything if it was wrapped in or dusted with nori. Here the broccoli is sautéed in fragrant sesame oil, but not so much that it loses its vibrancy or crunch. When I first made it, I crushed the kids' roasted nori snacks on top and sprinkled it with sesame seeds. Shockingly they devoured it, and as per usual, I stood at the kitchen counter eating the stray leftovers from their plates. I started adding sugar snap peas to test my luck, which didn't fare so well with the boys, but they still love broccoli prepared this way. When I'm making this for less finicky palates, the peas always find their way back in, usually to much applause and delight.

SERVES 4 TO 6

2 tablespoons **toasted sesame oil**

1 tablespoon **avocado oil**

1 head **broccoli**, cut into bite-size pieces (about 4 cups)

2 cups **sugar snap peas**, trimmed

¼ teaspoon **fine sea salt**

1 tablespoon **low-sodium tamari**

2 teaspoons **sesame seeds**

1 to 2 tablespoons **crushed toasted nori**

1. In a large skillet, heat the sesame oil and avocado oil over medium-high heat. Add the broccoli, sugar snap peas, and salt, and cook until the vegetables are bright green and tender, 5 to 7 minutes, adding a tablespoon of water if needed to prevent the pan from browning. The vegetables should be cooked through but still crispy.

2. Add the tamari and cook until the tamari is slightly reduced, 1 minute more. Remove the pan from the heat.

3. Sprinkle the sesame seeds and nori on top and serve hot.

Coconut Maple Roasted Kabocha Squash

A friend once called kabocha squash "queen of the season," and that is how I refer to it to this day. Squash season isn't universally celebrated, and I get it, because I didn't always love squash. But as I got older and learned how to properly season and roast it, my feelings changed, and we now have a deep love affair. When the first kabocha squash arrive at my favorite stall at the farmers' market, I show up early and load my basket. I promptly bring them home to wash and slice them and prepare a big batch of this. You want to make sure that the kabocha is well-coated in coconut oil (ghee also works very well here) and then lightly drizzle it with maple syrup just to bring out the sweet, tender notes and achieve that dreamy caramelization. I eat this for breakfast in yogurt bowls, or I serve it for dinner with a big pile of wilted greens, a nutty brown-rice dish, and some broiled tofu—there is truly no greater vegetarian weeknight dinner.

SERVES 4 TO 6

1 large (about 3 pounds) **kabocha squash**

2 tablespoons **coconut oil**, melted

2 tablespoons **pure maple syrup**

1 teaspoon **garlic powder**

½ teaspoon **fine sea salt**

1. Preheat the oven to 425°F. Line a baking sheet with parchment paper.

2. Cut the squash in half lengthwise and scrape out the seeds. Lay the squash cut-side down and slice into 1-inch half-moons. Place the slices on the prepared baking sheet and drizzle with the coconut oil, maple syrup, garlic powder, and salt. Using your hands or a spoon, toss until the slices are fully coated. Roast until the squash is tender when poked with a fork, 35 to 40 minutes (if using a conventional—not convection—oven, use a spatula to flip the squash at the 20-minute mark). If not serving immediately, let the squash cool, then store in an airtight container in the refrigerator for up to 3 days.

OG Vegetable Stir-Fry

WITH GINGER PEANUT DRESSING

When I was living in Colorado in my twenties and teaching snowboarding, a few friends would usually gather around my kitchen counter after work each day. We were all hungry, tired, and freezing, and none of them knew how to cook, let alone cook something healthy and nourishing. Even then, my fridge was always stocked with fresh, washed produce, and a stir-fry was the easiest way to put it to use. I would scoop a spoonful of peanut butter from the jar and add it to the wok once the vegetables were done cooking. This was probably one of the experiences that led me to open my first Spring Café in Aspen a few years later. A lot has changed since those days—now I eat this sitting at the counter with my three kids instead of three friends, but I still scoop the peanut butter straight from the jar and into the wok, because simple always wins, and if the stir-fry ain't broke . . .

SERVES 4 TO 6

1 (14-ounce) package **firm tofu**, drained and patted dry

4 tablespoons **low-sodium tamari**

3 tablespoons **avocado oil**

1 small **red onion**, sliced

½ head **green cabbage**, shredded (about 4 cups)

¼ head **red cabbage**, shredded (about 2 cups)

2 small **zucchini**, halved lengthwise and cut into ½-inch half moons

1 head **broccoli**, cut into bite-size pieces (about 4 cups)

2 **carrots**, grated

3 **garlic cloves**, smashed

1 (1-inch) piece **fresh ginger**, peeled

¼ teaspoon **fine sea salt** (optional)

2 tablespoons creamy **peanut butter**

Juice of ½ **lemon**

1 bunch **scallions**, thinly sliced

2 teaspoons **sesame seeds**

1. Cut the tofu into 1-inch pieces and place in a large bowl. Toss the tofu with 2 tablespoons of the tamari.

2. In a large skillet, heat 2 tablespoons of the avocado oil over medium-high heat. Add the marinated tofu and cook, flipping as needed every 4 to 5 minutes, until all the sides are evenly browned and crispy. Transfer the tofu to a plate.

3. In the same skillet, heat the remaining 1 tablespoon avocado oil and add the onion. Sauté for 2 minutes until slightly translucent. Add the green cabbage, red cabbage, zucchini, broccoli, carrots, and 2 tablespoons of water. Cook, stirring frequently, until the vegetables are slightly tender but retain their color, 3 to 4 minutes.

4. Add the smashed garlic cloves to the pan. Using a Microplane, grate the ginger into the vegetables and stir again. Stir in the remaining 2 tablespoons tamari and cook until the liquid is reduced and absorbed into the vegetables, about 1 minute. Taste for seasoning, and season with the salt, if desired.

5. Create a well in the center of the pan. Place the peanut butter in the well with 2 tablespoons water. Remove the pan from the heat, cover, and let stand for 2 minutes to melt the peanut butter. Lift the lid and add the tofu, then stir the peanut butter into the vegetables and tofu. Add the lemon juice, scallions, and sesame seeds and toss to combine. Serve immediately.

Cucumbers

WITH SEA SALT AND LIME

This dish is a staple in Central American cuisine and my favorite way to eat cucumbers. My middle son takes after me and requests this daily in his lunch box. If you have a child who doesn't love green vegetables, try this. It's also a delicious topping for taco night, a perfect accompaniment to nachos or quesadillas, and a refreshing salad on its own. If you like spice, a little chile or red pepper flakes does wonders here.

SERVES 4

6 small **Persian cucumbers**, chopped

½ teaspoon **fine sea salt**

Juice of 2 **limes**

In a large bowl, season the cucumbers with the salt and lime juice and toss to fully coat. Serve immediately, or store in an airtight container in the refrigerator for up to 3 days.

Crunchy Cabbage Slaw

I love cabbage and have always wanted to love coleslaw, but I usually find it too sugary and mayonnaise laden. In this version, I massage the cabbage until it's just tender enough to enjoy, and I omit the sugar and add a little apple cider vinegar, olive oil, and lime juice to keep it crunchy and tart. If this is sacrilege to you, you could use a vegan or egg-based mayo, but in my humble opinion a mayo-free slaw is the way to go. Surprisingly all three of my kids have loved this since they started really eating solid foods, so I usually make a big batch to store in the refrigerator and pull it out as a reliable accompaniment to sandwiches, pastas, and quesadillas on the otherwise veggie-less plates of little eaters.

SERVES 6 TO 8

½ head **green cabbage**, thinly sliced

½ head **red cabbage**, thinly sliced

½ cup minced **fresh chives**

1 **carrot**, grated

½ cup **extra-virgin olive oil**

¼ cup **apple cider vinegar**

Juice of 2 **limes**

½ teaspoon **fine sea salt**

1. In a large bowl, mix together the green and red cabbage until evenly distributed. Mix in the chives and carrot. Using your hands, toss and massage the vegetables together until they begin to release some of their water and break down. This will take 2 to 3 minutes and may marry their colors slightly, and that's okay!

2. In a small bowl, whisk together the olive oil, vinegar, lime juice, and salt. Pour the dressing over the slaw and toss until the vegetables are fully coated. Serve immediately, or store an airtight container in the refrigerator for up to 3 days.

Baked French Fries

We are a family of french fry lovers, and we usually eat them two or three times per week. It might be concerning except that most of the time we make fries at home using this method, so I can feel good about my kids (and me) chowing down on them. The trick with homemade fries is to soak them in an ice bath to remove some of the starch, a tip I learned on Instagram ages ago and now swear by. Russet potatoes work best here. If you want crispy baked fries, you need to carefully lay them on a baking sheet and let them bake without disturbing them, other than rotating the baking sheet once midway. The final product is light, crispy, and always a hit.

SERVES 4 TO 6

5 large **russet potatoes**, peeled

1 tablespoon **avocado oil**

1 teaspoon **sweet paprika**

½ teaspoon **garlic powder**

½ teaspoon **onion powder**

¼ teaspoon **fine sea salt**

1. Preheat the oven to 375°F.

2. Fill a large bowl with ice and water. Cut the potatoes lengthwise into ¼-inch-thick slices, then cut each slice lengthwise into ¼-inch-thick batons that resemble traditional french fries. Place the potatoes in the ice water and soak for 20 minutes to release starch.

3. Drain the potatoes and pat them dry. Scatter them on a large baking sheet and season with the avocado oil, paprika, garlic powder, onion powder, and salt. Using your hands or a wooden spoon, toss to fully coat the potatoes and rearrange them into a single layer.

4. Bake until the potatoes are crispy and browned, rotating the baking sheet halfway through, 40 to 45 minutes. Allow them to cool slightly before enjoying.

Roasted Stuffed Acorn Squash

WITH COCONUT RICE, MUSHROOMS, AND GOLDEN RAISINS

I think a lot of people get hung up wondering how and if vegetables can be filling enough for an entire meal. This is one of those dishes I make for the most skeptical of carnivores when they come to my house for dinner. This stuffed squash checks all the boxes of a hearty, filling, and delicious vegetable dish. The mushrooms add a little umami and, dare I say, meaty flavor. The squash is perfectly tender and not too sweet, and this coconut rice would honestly make any carnivore a believer. Because you can cook the rice ahead and the squash takes very little prep time, this is an excellent recipe to make for a dinner party. I promise, no one will leave hungry or disappointed.

SERVES 4

4 **acorn squash**

4 tablespoons **avocado oil**, plus more for greasing

1 teaspoon **smoked paprika**

1 teaspoon **garlic powder**

1 teaspoon **onion powder**

¾ teaspoon **fine sea salt**

2 cups full-fat **coconut milk**

1 cup **uncooked jasmine rice**, soaked overnight in water and rinsed

½ cup **golden raisins**

¼ cup chopped **fresh flat-leaf parsley**

8 ounces **shiitake mushrooms**, chopped

2 tablespoons **low-sodium tamari**

1. Preheat the oven to 425°F. Grease a 9 × 13-inch or similar-size baking dish with avocado oil.

2. Remove the tops from the acorn squash and scoop out the seeds. Place the squash in the baking dish, cut-side up. If necessary, slice a small amount off the bottom of each of the squash so that they can sit upright in the baking dish. Evenly drizzle 3 tablespoons of the avocado oil on top of the squash, then evenly season them with the paprika, garlic powder, onion powder, and ½ teaspoon of the salt.

3. Roast the squash for 30 minutes, or until softened but not yet tender.

4. While the squash is roasting, place the coconut milk and rice in a saucepan and bring to a simmer over medium-high heat. Reduce the heat to medium-low, cover, and cook for 10 minutes, or until the rice has fully absorbed the coconut milk. Remove the pot from the heat and allow the rice to steam, covered, for 10 minutes. Fluff the rice and stir in the raisins and parsley.

5. In a large skillet, heat the remaining 1 tablespoon avocado oil over medium-high heat. Add the mushrooms and tamari and cook until the mushrooms are browned and reduced in size by about half, 3 to 4 minutes. Add the mushrooms to the coconut rice and season the mixture with the remaining ¼ teaspoon of the salt.

6. Evenly divide the rice mixture among the acorn squash cavities and return the squash to the oven. Roast for 30 minutes more, then remove from the oven and let cool slightly before serving.

Sizzling Baby Bok Choy

WITH FRESH GINGER

We're a kale-, chard-, and spinach-obsessed society, and that's fine, but Asian greens like bok choy offer supreme texture and flavor and are highly alkaline and easy to digest. Unlike its American cousins, bok choy doesn't contain high amounts of oxalic acid, making it an especially perfect first green vegetable for babies and young children. All that aside, it's just straight up delicious. If chopped small and overcooked, however, it can turn mushy and slimy, so keeping the whole bulb and leaves intact helps maintain the crisp texture, especially when you buy the baby ones. I love this method of searing them in avocado oil with loads of fresh ginger, another staple in Asian home cooking. My kids call this dish "knife and fork" bok choy, which it is. It's become a frequent staple on our family table when baby bok choy is in season at the farmers' market.

SERVES 4 TO 6

3 tablespoons **avocado oil**

6 to 8 heads **baby bok choy**, halved

1 (1-inch) piece **fresh ginger**, peeled and grated

2 **garlic cloves**, grated

Juice of 1 **lime**

1. In a large skillet, heat 1 tablespoon of the avocado oil over medium-high heat. Add about a third of the bok choy, cut-side down. Cook for 2 to 3 minutes, until the bok choy has browned. Flip the bok choy and cook for 1 minute more, then transfer the seared bok choy to a plate. Repeat one more time, using another tablespoon of avocado oil and another third of the bok choy.

2. Add the remaining 1 tablespoon avocado oil and the last third of bok choy to the skillet. Cook until the bok choy starts to brown, 2 to 3 minutes, then flip the bok choy, add the ginger and garlic, and cook until fragrant, about 1 minute more. Add the lime juice and 1 tablespoon water to deglaze the pan. Transfer the sizzling bok choy to the plate with the seared bok choy from the previous rounds, pour the pan sauce over them, and serve.

Sautéed Radicchio

WITH CHICKPEAS

One of the first meals I made my husband was penne with wilted radicchio and chickpeas, which he still asks for to this day. Most people think of radicchio as a salad green and don't realize that it can be sautéed, braised, or stewed to bring down the bitterness. This is the kind of recipe that makes you feel like you've put something beautiful together, even if you just want dinner for one on a cozy night in. Serving it with or without penne is up to you, so long as you don't forget the drizzle of sweet balsamic and tart lemon at the end.

SERVES 4 TO 6

3 tablespoons **avocado oil**

1 (13-ounce) jar **chickpeas**, such as Jovial, or 1 (15-ounce) can, rinsed and drained

3 **garlic cloves**, chopped

¼ teaspoon **fine sea salt**

2 heads **radicchio**, chopped

2 tablespoons **low-sodium tamari**

Zest and juice of ½ **lemon**

1 teaspoon **balsamic vinegar**

1. In a large skillet, heat the avocado oil over medium-high heat. Add the chickpeas, garlic, and salt and cook, stirring occasionally, for 3 to 4 minutes, until the garlic is fragrant and the chickpeas are slightly crispy.

2. Add the radicchio and stir to combine with the chickpea mixture. Cook, stirring occasionally, until the radicchio has reduced in size by about half, 3 to 4 minutes.

3. Add the tamari, lemon zest, lemon juice, balsamic vinegar, and 1 tablespoon water. Stir to combine and serve while warm.

Petite Japanese Sweet Potatoes

WITH MISO BUTTER

One of my favorite restaurants was a Japanese place in Venice, California, called MTN. It was produce-forward, with hints of macrobiotic cooking methods, and the menu had a lot of vegetarian options. The best thing they made were small Japanese sweet potatoes that were roasted, quartered, and drizzled in some kind of magical miso butter—even just writing that leaves me with a deep nostalgia. When MTN closed and I realized I'd never have the original again, I made it my mission to achieve something similar. If you can, go the extra mile and whip the butter and sweet white miso paste with an electric mixer; I haven't been able to achieve the fluffiness by hand. The touch of maple syrup brings out the supreme sweetness of the potatoes, and the closest I got to the original dish was when I used unsalted butter. Nothing will ever compare to the MTN Japanese sweet potatoes, but this is my humble homage to a very special and greatly missed dish and restaurant.

■ **SERVES 6**

6 **baby Japanese sweet potatoes**

4 tablespoons (½ stick) **unsalted butter**, at room temperature

1 tablespoon **white miso paste**

1 tablespoon **pure maple syrup**

1. Preheat the oven to 425°F.

2. Using a fork, poke the sweet potatoes a few times and place on a baking sheet. Roast the potatoes for 60 to 90 minutes, until the potato is tender when pierced with a knife.

3. While the potatoes are roasting, in the bowl of a stand mixer fitted with the whisk attachment or in a large bowl using a handheld mixer, beat together the butter, miso, and maple syrup on medium speed until light and fluffy, about 2 minutes.

4. Remove the potatoes from the oven and let cool slightly. When they are cool enough to handle (but still warm), split the top of each sweet potato, squeeze from the ends to expose the potato flesh and evenly top with the miso butter. Serve warm.

Sandwiches, Wraps, Etc.

I Love a Hoagie Night

When people begin to think about eating healthy, they usually think they have to give up things like big sandwiches made with delicious crusty sourdough and stuffed with decadent fillings. I'm here to disprove that myth. Sandwiches and, in particular, hoagies are one of my favorite food groups. Even my mom, the original health nut, was a huge fan of sandwiches, and her creations were legendary among my friends who came over after school. In our house, hoagie night was a sacred tradition. I love any meal that has a choose-your-own-adventure vibe, and there is no better vehicle for this than a hoagie. The combination of creamy bright pesto and tender roasted portobello caps never fails. I set out all the toppings on the counter and let the kids or our guests assemble their own. I've given you a few ideas, like sun-dried tomatoes, artichokes, and goat cheese, but feel free to add anything you like. It could be a strong Dijon, roasted summer squash, and other types of cheese. The goal is to make it your own, make it delicious, and make it fun! And if you still don't believe me that eating healthy can be decadent and delicious, or that vegetables make a great hoagie, don't take my word for it—take a bite and see.

SERVES 4 TO 6

2 bunches **basil**

2 tablespoons **pine nuts**, toasted

2 tablespoons **extra-virgin olive oil**

Juice of 1 **lemon**

2 **garlic cloves**, peeled

¼ teaspoon **fine sea salt**

1 tablespoon **avocado oil**

6 to 8 **portobello mushroom caps**, sliced

1 tablespoon **low-sodium tamari**

1 large **baguette**, toasted, if desired

1 cup halved **marinated artichoke hearts**

½ cup sliced oil-packed **sun-dried tomatoes**

¼ pound **hard goat cheese**, sliced

1 cup **arugula**

1. In a blender or food processor, combine the basil, pine nuts, olive oil, lemon juice, 1 of the garlic cloves, and the salt. Blend on high speed until the mixture is fully blended and creamy. This will yield about ¾ cup pesto. It can be made up to 1 week in advance and stored in an airtight container in the refrigerator.

2. In a large skillet, heat the avocado oil over medium-high heat. Cook the mushrooms until they're reduced in size by about a third and are browned and tender, 5 to 7 minutes. Reduce the heat to low and add the tamari. Using a Microplane, grate the remaining garlic clove into the pan and stir to combine. Remove from the heat and cool.

3. To assemble the sandwich, slice the baguette lengthwise and evenly divide the pesto between the top and bottom, spreading to cover both sides entirely. To the bottom slice, evenly distribute the cooked portobello mushrooms, followed by the artichoke hearts, sun-dried tomatoes, cheese, and arugula. Sandwich the baguette and cut into 4 or 6 pieces.

Black Bean Quesadillas

WITH CARAMELIZED ONION, ZUCCHINI, AND GOAT'S-MILK CHEDDAR

This recipes feels so simple, but it's also delicious, quick, and intuitive for any level of home chef. A quesadilla is a magic food, meaning you can stuff almost anything between two tortillas, include some cheese, and sear it in an oiled pan, and it's very hard for it to not be delicious. I also find that, as is the case with tacos, kids will eat almost anything if it's inside of a quesadilla. The first time I made these was when one of my best friends, Taryn, came over with her family for an early dinner. We love to cook together, and she had an idea for an onion and zucchini quesadilla. I had a tub of stewed black beans to use up and some goat cheddar in the fridge. We combined forces and whipped these up for our combined six kids and all the adults, and every morsel was eaten. Now it's my go-to combination for quesadilla night. Don't forget the guacamole, pico, and sour cream to make them even more delicious! Quesadillas are also a great way to use up leftovers—if you have cooked veggies or beans getting sad in your refrigerator, throw them into a quesadilla!

SERVES 4

2 tablespoons plus 4 teaspoons **avocado oil**

1 small **yellow onion**, thinly sliced

1 small **fennel bulb**, thinly sliced

½ teaspoon **fine sea salt**

2 small **zucchini**, chopped

3 **scallions**, thinly sliced

1 cup **baby spinach**

8 **grain-free tortillas**, such as Siete Foods

1 (13-ounce) jar **black beans**, such as Jovial, or 1 (15-ounce) can, drained, rinsed, and mashed; or 1 cup cooked black beans, mashed

8 tablespoons shredded **goat's-milk cheddar cheese**

For Serving (Optional)

Go-to Guacamole (page 39)

Pico de Gallo (page 40)

Dairy-free sour cream

1. In a large skillet, heat 2 tablespoons of the avocado oil over medium heat. Add the onion and fennel and season with ¼ teaspoon of the salt. Cook, stirring occasionally, until the onion is slightly translucent, about 5 minutes.

2. Add the zucchini to the skillet and stir to combine. Cook until the zucchini is slightly translucent and tender but still has some bite, 2 to 3 minutes. Add the scallions, spinach, and remaining ¼ teaspoon salt and cook until the spinach is wilted, about 2 minutes more. Transfer the veggies to a bowl.

3. Lay one tortilla on a flat surface and add 2 tablespoons of the mashed beans on top. Spread one-quarter (about 1 cup) of the veggie mixture on the beans and scatter 2 tablespoons of the cheese on top. Place another tortilla over the cheese. Repeat the process with the remaining tortillas and fillings.

4. Wipe out the skillet you used for the veggies and, in it, heat 1 teaspoon of the avocado oil over medium-high heat. Once hot, add one of the prepared quesadillas to the pan and cook until the tortilla is golden brown on the bottom, 2 to 3 minutes. Carefully flip the quesadilla and cook until the other side is golden brown, 2 to 3 minutes more. Remove the quesadilla from the pan and repeat the process with the remaining quesadillas, adding another teaspoon of avocado oil to the pan before adding each uncooked quesadilla.

5. Allow the quesadillas to cool slightly and slice them into halves or quarters. Serve with guacamole, pico de gallo, and/or sour cream.

Spicy Avocado Miso Caesar Wrap

This wrap is for those days when you have ten minutes to make lunch and five minutes to eat it, but you still want to make something nutrient-dense and feel great afterward. This is also a reminder that healthy food doesn't have to be tedious. I frequently make this on very hectic days before school pickup and take it with me on my walk to school or eat it at the kitchen counter while I finish up my work. Miso is the secret ingredient to any good vegan Caesar dressing, and the red pepper flakes add the perfect amount of punch. Some of you might read this and think, "But it's just veggies! Where's the protein?!" And yes, you can add tofu or another type of protein, but I hope meals like this help retrain your mind a little when it comes to counting protein and other macronutrients. A pile of plants and healthy fats (hello, avocado) is one of the healthiest and most satisfying things you can put in your body!

MAKES 2 WRAPS

1 to 2 heads **romaine lettuce**, thinly sliced (about 6 cups)

1 ripe **avocado**, diced

¼ cup pitted **green olives**, such as Castelvetrano, coarsely chopped

¼ cup **extra-virgin olive oil**

2 tablespoons **apple cider vinegar**

1 tablespoon **white miso paste**

Juice of ½ **lemon**

¼ teaspoon **red pepper flakes**

¼ teaspoon **fine sea salt**

2 large **grain-free tortillas**, such as Siete Foods

1. In a large bowl, combine the romaine, avocado, and olives.

2. In a small bowl, whisk together the olive oil, vinegar, miso, lemon juice, red pepper flakes, and salt. Pour the dressing over the salad and toss to fully coat.

3. To assemble each wrap, if you have an electric range, turn a stovetop burner on low heat and set one of the tortillas directly on the burner. Cook for 30 seconds and flip. This will soften and slightly char the wrap. (If you have a gas range, you can do this in a skillet.) Repeat with the second tortilla. Lay each tortilla on a flat surface and evenly divide the salad mixture between the two. Roll up the tortillas and slice in half. Serve immediately or make ahead, wrap in parchment paper, and store in the refrigerator for up to 6 hours to enjoy later as a packed lunch or picnic.

A Classic Tempeh Reuben

If I were a meat eater, I'd probably eat a Reuben every day. Maybe it's my Jewish heritage or my NYC upbringing or my love of delis, but this hearty pressed sandwich on rye with Russian dressing, melted cheese, and sauerkraut sounds like the ultimate chef's kiss. I'll admit that I've never actually tried a real Reuben with corned beef, but I did grow up on the tempeh variety. This sandwich was one of our first hero items on Spring Café's menu in Aspen. It has jammy caramelized peppers, a generous slathering of our Thousand Island dressing (a mix of vegan mayo and ketchup), and a heaping pile of sauerkraut. Tempeh is one of the healthiest forms of soy because it's fermented and minimally processed; it's also an excellent source of protein and easy to digest. Sometimes when I'm stumped on what to make for dinner and my go-to recipes aren't hitting the spot, I make a few of these—vegetarian comfort food at its finest.

MAKES 2 SANDWICHES

1 (8-ounce) package **tempeh**

4 tablespoons **Ginger-Tamari Dressing** (page 32)

2 teaspoons **avocado oil**

1 **red bell pepper**, sliced

3 tablespoons **vegan mayo**, such as Vegenaise

1 tablespoon **ketchup**

4 slices **gluten-free sandwich bread**, toasted

½ **avocado**, sliced

4 heaping tablespoons **sauerkraut**

1. Cut the tempeh in half and place it in a medium bowl with 2 tablespoons of the ginger tamari sauce. Allow the mixture to marinate for 15 minutes.

2. Meanwhile, in a medium skillet, heat 1 teaspoon of the avocado oil over medium-high heat. Add the pepper and cook, stirring occasionally, until tender and slightly browned. Reduce the heat to low and add the remaining 2 tablespoons ginger tamari sauce. Stir the sauce into the pepper and cook until the liquid is absorbed, about 1 minute. Transfer the pepper to a plate to cool.

3. Add the remaining 1 teaspoon avocado oil to the pan and return the heat to medium-high. Drain the tempeh and place the pieces in the skillet. Cook the tempeh for 3 to 4 minutes per side, or until golden brown all over. Remove the tempeh from the pan.

4. In a small bowl, mixture together the vegan mayo and ketchup.

5. To assemble the sandwiches, add 1 tablespoon of the mayo-ketchup mixture to one side of each piece of bread. Place a piece of the tempeh on each of two slices of the bread, and top evenly with the pepper. Divide the avocado slices and sauerkraut between both sandwiches and top each with a second slice of bread. If desired, cut each sandwich in half before serving.

Curried Tempeh Salad Lettuce Cups

When I was writing this book, there was a chicken salad craze going viral on Instagram. Chicken salad of every kind dominated my feed and made me, who doesn't particularly enjoy chicken, crave a chicken salad. One caught my eye that was curried and filled with celery and raisins, and it got to the point one day where I just had to make something similar. I set out to make a curried tempeh salad and didn't have the highest expectations, but WOW did this recipe deliver! I had some Bibb lettuce on hand, so I made little cups and put them out for lunch. Our whole family agreed it was a hit!

SERVES 2 TO 4

2 tablespoons **avocado oil**

1 (8-ounce) package **tempeh**, chopped

2 tablespoons **low-sodium tamari**

3 **celery stalks**, minced

1 **carrot**, minced

½ cup **raisins**

¼ cup **vegan mayo**, such as Vegenaise

1 tablespoon **Dijon mustard**

1 tablespoon **curry powder**

1 tablespoon **smoked paprika**

¼ teaspoon **fine sea salt**

2 tablespoons chopped **fresh flat-leaf parsley**

1 head **Bibb lettuce**, leaves separated

1. In a large skillet, heat the avocado oil over medium heat. Add the tempeh and cook, undisturbed, until it begins to brown, 2 to 3 minutes. Season with the tamari, flip, and cook until the tamari is absorbed and the tempeh is fully browned, 2 to 3 minutes more.

2. In a large bowl, combine the celery and carrot. Add the vegan mayo, mustard, curry powder, paprika, salt, and parsley and mix to combine. Fold in the warm tempeh and mix well until all the ingredients are fully combined.

3. Spoon the tempeh mixture into lettuce wraps and serve immediately. The mixture can be made in advance and stored separately from the lettuce in an airtight container in the refrigerator for up to 3 days.

Pastas & Noodles

Ramen Noodles

WITH ASIAN GREENS

I go wild for ramen noodles, and my family does too. Luckily there are some brands that make a delicious gluten-free version so we're able to satisfy our craving a few days a week. This is a twist on the Japanese classic: I omit the broth and turn it into more of a stir-fry, but sometimes when it's freezing out, I make a miso base and turn this into more of a traditional ramen bowl. I strongly urge you to try Asian greens here like tatsoi or Chinese broccoli, which are mild and tender and perfect for the delicate ramen noodles. I love to brown some tofu and toss it in at the end. The arrowroot starch helps to naturally thicken the sauce like cornstarch would, but if you prefer a thinner, brothier effect you can easily omit it. Whenever my kids are under the weather or we all just need a cozy meal in, this is our go-to. There's really no problem that a homemade ramen bowl can't solve.

SERVES 4 TO 6

10 ounces **gluten-free ramen,** such as Lotus Foods

2 tablespoons **low-sodium tamari**

2 tablespoons **toasted sesame oil**

3 tablespoons **avocado oil**

Zest and juice of 1 **lime**

1 teaspoon **arrowroot starch**

1 **garlic clove**, peeled

1 (1-inch) piece **fresh ginger,** peeled

1 **red bell pepper**, thinly sliced

1 **yellow bell pepper**, thinly sliced

¼ head **napa cabbage**, thinly sliced (about 2 cups)

2 heads **bok choy**, or 4 to 6 heads baby bok choy, thinly sliced (about 4 cups)

1. Cook the ramen according to the package instructions and drain.

2. In a small bowl, whisk together the tamari, sesame oil, 2 tablespoons of the avocado oil, the lime zest and juice, and the arrowroot starch. Grate the garlic and ginger into the sauce.

3. In a large skillet or wok, heat the remaining 1 tablespoon avocado oil over medium-high heat. Add the red and yellow bell peppers and cook until the peppers are slightly blistered and reduced in volume, 2 to 3 minutes. Add the cabbage and bok choy and stir them into the peppers. Cook, stirring occasionally, until the vegetables are slightly softened but retain their bright color, 2 to 3 minutes more.

4. Reduce the heat to low and stir in the tamari sauce and ramen. Cook until the mixture is fully combined and the sauce has reduced and been absorbed into the vegetables and noodles, about 1 minute. Serve immediately.

One-Pot Orzo

WITH SPINACH, WHITE BEANS, AND BURST SUNGOLDS

This is my favorite meal to make on a rainy and cool summer or fall night when Sungold tomatoes are at their peak. I love risotto but admittedly don't have the patience to stand at the stove and take the time necessary to cook it properly; enter orzo. Orzo is a little more forgiving than Arborio rice and doesn't get mushy when you want to make a brothier one-pot dish with a risotto-like vibe. I start this on the stove, and it comes out like a jammy, delicious casserole. I'm a gluten-free girl 90 percent of the time, but orzo is one place where I prefer the original because the GF versions I've found just don't have the same consistency, plus I really love orzo. That said, I've tested this recipe both ways, and liquid and cooking time will vary depending on whether you choose gluten-free or traditional orzo. Either way, this is utterly delicious, offers an easy cleanup, and is great for feeding a group. And because of the Sungolds and the vibrant spinach, it's beautiful too!

SERVES 4 TO 6

2 tablespoons **avocado oil**

1 small **yellow onion**, diced

1½ teaspoons **fine sea salt,** plus more if needed

1 pint **Sungold tomatoes**

1 pound **orzo**

1 (13-ounce) jar **white beans**, such as Jovial, or 1 (15-ounce) can, rinsed and drained

3 cups **baby spinach**

1. In a large Dutch oven, heat the avocado oil over medium-high heat. Add the onion and ½ teaspoon of the salt and cook, stirring occasionally, until the onion is translucent, 5 to 7 minutes. Add the tomatoes and cook until the tomatoes begin to burst, about 5 minutes more. Stir in the orzo and cook for 1 minute more to toast the orzo.

2. Reduce the heat to low and add 3 cups water, the beans, spinach, and remaining 1 teaspoon salt. Cook, stirring occasionally to distribute the water and prevent the orzo from sticking to the bottom of the pot, until the orzo is tender and the liquid has been absorbed, 15 minutes. Season with additional salt, if desired, and serve warm.

STAUB
STAUB

Grandma Hazel's Noodle Kugel

Kugel is one of my favorite dishes of all time. I understand if you raise your eyebrows at this declaration—a dish made with egg noodles, golden raisins, and crushed cornflakes is not exactly my signature, but hear me out. My love for sweet noodle kugel is thanks in part to my grandmother Hazel, who lived to age 106 and instilled in me a deep joy of cooking and life. Whenever she made this dish, it seemed to get even more delicious. When I grew up and became the family member who hosted holidays and other gatherings, I begged my grandmother to write down her recipe, which had been passed down from her mother, Bella. But hers was made from memory with a "pinch of sugar here" and a "dollop of sour cream there." At least once a year, I make Hazel's original version, using real dairy and adding cottage cheese, but otherwise I use vegan dairy, as here, and it really spares none of the flavor or deliciousness.

SERVES 6 TO 8

8 tablespoons (1 stick) **unsalted butter or vegan butter**, melted and cooled, plus more for greasing

Fine sea salt

2 (9-ounce) packages **gluten-free brown-rice egg tagliatelle**, such as Jovial

5 large **eggs**

1 cup **dairy-free sour cream**, such as Forager Project

½ cup unsweetened **plant-based plain yogurt**

1 cup unsweetened **oat milk**

1½ cups **coconut sugar or pure maple sugar**

1 tablespoon **ground cinnamon**

1 teaspoon **pure vanilla extract**

4 cups **fruit juice–sweetened cornflakes**, such as Nature's Path

1 cup **golden raisins**

1. Preheat the oven to 350° F. Grease a 9 × 13-inch or similar-size baking dish with butter.

2. Bring a large pot of salted water to a boil over high heat. Add the noodles and cook until al dente according to the package instructions and drain.

3. In a high-speed blender or food processor, combine the eggs, sour cream, yogurt, oat milk, 4 tablespoons of the melted butter, 1 cup of the coconut sugar, the cinnamon, and the vanilla. Blend on high speed until well combined, about 2 minutes.

4. In a large bowl, combine the cornflakes, the remaining 4 tablespoons melted butter, and the remaining ½ cup coconut sugar. Using your hands, crush the cornflakes and mix until well combined.

5. Place the noodles in the prepared baking dish. Evenly distribute the raisins over the noodles and then pour the egg mixture on top. Evenly top with the cornflake mixture, covering all the noodles. Bake until the kugel is firm and nicely browned, 55 to 60 minutes. If the top browns too quickly, cover it with parchment paper and then seal it with aluminum foil. Let cool for 10 minutes to set. Serve warm or at room temperature.

NOTE: To prepare this in advance, bake fully, cool, and cover with parchment and then plastic wrap. Store in the refrigerator for up to 2 days in advance. On the day of serving, remove from the refrigerator, top the kugel with the cornflakes and bake at 325°F for 30 minutes or until the top is golden brown.

Stuffed Shells

WITH TOFU RICOTTA

This is a recipe that brings up a lot of core memories from my youth, which just goes to show that food is about so much more than just what's on our plates. It's about nourishment, connection, and remembrance. This meal instantly transports me to my childhood kitchen, watching my mom make tofu ricotta and then helping her stuff each shell before slathering them in a generous helping of her homemade marinara. I loved this dish so much as a kid because it felt so decadent and special, even though my mom often made it on weeknights for family dinner; and let's face it, shapes like giant pasta shells just make food more fun. The classic version of this dish has mozzarella or ricotta baked on top, so you have some choices here. You can dot tofu ricotta on top of the sauce before you bake to give it a creamier base (that's my preferred method), or you can melt your favorite cheese on top until it's brown and bubbling. It's delicious any way you choose to bake it, and I hope it becomes a core food memory for your family too.

SERVES 4 TO 6

8 ounces **brown-rice pasta shells**, such as Pasta Joy

1 (14-ounce) package **firm tofu**, drained and patted dry with paper towels

Leaves from 4 to 5 **thyme sprigs**

2 teaspoons **dried oregano**

1 teaspoon **garlic powder**

1 teaspoon **onion powder**

½ teaspoon **fine sea salt**, plus more for the pasta water

2½ cups **Slow-Roasted Chunky Tomato Sauce** (page 42) or store-bought marinara

1. Preheat the oven to 375°F.

2. Bring a large pot of generously salted water to a boil over high heat. Cook the pasta shells until al dente according to the package instructions and drain.

3. In a food processor, combine the tofu, thyme, oregano, garlic powder, onion power, and salt. Pulse the ingredients until the texture resembles traditional ricotta cheese.

4. To assemble the stuffed shells, evenly spread ½ cup of the tomato sauce on the bottom of a 9 × 13-inch baking dish. Place the shells in the dish, open-sides up.

5. Fill each shell with 2 heaping tablespoons of the tofu ricotta, adding more as needed to use it all up. Evenly pour the remaining 2 cups tomato sauce over the shells. (The shells will not be fully coated.)

6. Cover the dish with a layer of parchment and then a layer of aluminum foil. Bake for 25 minutes, or until the sauce is bubbly. Remove from the oven and allow the shells to cool slightly before serving.

Penne alla Norma (Sorta)

One of my favorite Italian restaurants has an eggplant pasta that I literally dream about. The eggplant is caramelized and tender, and the rich red sauce is garlicky and perfect. They include chunks of mozzarella cheese, which I ask them to omit. I decided I wanted to make a version at home using my Slow-Roasted Chunky Tomato Sauce and with soft goat cheese in lieu of mozzarella. I use smaller eggplants, which tend to be sweeter and don't require you to salt them and remove the excess water before you roast them, because let's be real, what working mom of three has time to salt her eggplants?! If you can't tolerate any dairy but you want to achieve the same effect as the traditional dish, try it with cashew mozzarella. I love serving this at a dinner party with a huge green salad and crusty bread for scooping up all the extra roasted tomato sauce and bits of caramelized eggplant at the bottom of the bowl.

SERVES 4 TO 6

2 pounds small **eggplant**, diced

2 tablespoons **extra-virgin olive oil**

½ teaspoon **fine sea salt**, plus more for the pasta water

1 pound **penne pasta**

4 cups **Slow-Roasted Chunky Tomato Sauce** (page 42), or 1 (32-ounce) jar **tomato sauce**

8 to 10 ounces **goat cheese**

1. Preheat the oven to 325°F.

2. Spread the eggplant in a single layer over a baking sheet. Season it with the olive oil and salt and roast for 1 hour, or until the eggplant is browned and tastes sweet and is slightly chewy. Remove from the oven and prepare the pasta.

3. Bring a large pot of water to a boil and season generously with salt. Cook the penne according to the package instructions and drain.

4. Using the same pasta pot, heat the tomato sauce over low heat until bubbling. Add the pasta and eggplant and stir until all the ingredients are fully combined. Transfer to a large serving platter or individual seving dishes and crumble the goat cheese over the top, then serve.

Hearty Bean and Vegetable Shepherd's Pie

This vegetarian twist on shepherd's pie is decadent and luxurious. I use pinto beans in lieu of minced meat and load it with peas, carrots, celery, and herbs to keep it light and veggie focused. A good shepherd's pie should have a stewy consistency and shouldn't dry out in the oven. You can use vegetable broth here, but I always run out and just use water. The mashed potato crust is so rich and decadent and gets just the right amount of perfectly crispy once it bakes. If you have an ovenproof heavy-bottomed pot, you can sauté everything in that and then add the potatoes right on top instead of using a separate baking pan. This is so cozy and comforting on cold winter nights. Pair it with a big crisp green salad, and you're good to go!

SERVES 4 TO 6

2 tablespoons **avocado oil**, plus more for greasing

4 large **russet potatoes**, peeled and coarsely chopped

3 tablespoons **unsalted butter**, at room temperature

¼ cup unsweetened **nut milk**, at room temperature

¾ teaspoon **fine sea salt**

1 tablespoon chopped **fresh chives**

3 **celery stalks**, chopped

3 **carrots**, chopped

1 small **yellow onion**, chopped

1 teaspoon **dried thyme**

1 teaspoon **dried oregano**

1 (13-ounce) jar **pinto beans**, such as Jovial, or 1 (15-ounce) can, rinsed and drained

1 cup **frozen peas**

2 tablespoons **extra-virgin olive oil**

2 teaspoons **sweet paprika**

1. Preheat the oven to 375°F. Grease an 8-inch-square or similar-size ovenproof pan with avocado oil.

2. In a large pot, cover the potatoes with cold water and bring to a boil over medium-high heat. Cook until the potatoes are fork-tender, 12 to 15 minutes. Drain the potatoes and place in a large bowl to cool slightly.

3. While the potatoes are still warm, add the butter, milk, and ¼ teaspoon of the salt. Using a potato masher or large fork, mash the potatoes until they are light and fluffy and everything is completely incorporated. Fold in the chives.

4. In a large Dutch oven, heat the avocado oil over medium-high heat. Add the celery, carrots, onion, and ¼ teaspoon salt. Cook, stirring occasionally, until the vegetables are tender but still retain their bright color, 5 to 7 minutes.

5. Stir in the thyme and oregano and cook for 1 minute more. Stir in the beans and 2 cups water. Bring the liquid to a strong simmer. Reduce the heat to medium-low and simmer until the mixture has reduced by half, 10 to 15 minutes. Taste for seasoning and add the remaining ¼ teaspoon salt, if desired. Stir in the peas.

6. Transfer the vegetables to the prepared baking pan. Evenly distribute the mashed potatoes over the vegetables, covering the vegetables completely. Drizzle the potatoes with the olive oil and dust with the paprika. Pour 1 tablespoon water into each corner of the pan (this keeps the filling extra moist). Bake for about 40 minutes, until the potatoes are lightly browned. Remove from the oven and allow the shepherd's pie to cool slightly before serving. Leftovers can be covered and stored in the refrigerator for up to 3 days.

Tempeh Lentil Bolognese

What to make my kids for dinner is my Roman Empire. I also love having something simmering away on the stove for hours that makes my kitchen smell delicious; enter this vegan Bolognese. I love to make a batch on a Sunday afternoon and then enjoy it served over a big bowl of gluten-free pasta all week long. Usually I serve it heaped on top of a bowl of gluten-free pasta with some finely grated goat cheese, but I also eat it throughout the week for lunch without any accompaniment and it's equally as delicious. It's important to brown the tempeh and mushrooms separately, otherwise you'll wind up with a bland, mushy sauce, so the extra step—and the extra pan—is worth it! This is packed with plant protein and fiber, and I feel so good when I see my kids devour it. I've also made this for lovers of traditional Bolognese, and they all agree it's as good as the meat version. If you're looking for a crowd-pleasing way to introduce your family to meatless Mondays or you just want a simple and satisfying recipe that you can batch-cook and enjoy all week long, this is a great place to start.

SERVES 4 TO 6

4 tablespoons **avocado oil**

3 **carrots**, chopped

3 **celery stalks**, chopped

3 **garlic cloves**, chopped

1 **shallot**, chopped

½ teaspoon **fine sea salt**

2 teaspoons **dried oregano**

1 teaspoon **dried basil**

1 tablespoon **tomato paste**

1 (15-ounce) can **crushed tomatoes**

1 cup cooked **green lentils**

1 tablespoon **balsamic vinegar**

8 ounces **tempeh**

6 **shiitake mushroom caps**, thinly sliced

2 tablespoons **low-sodium tamari**

1. In a large Dutch oven, heat 2 tablespoons of the avocado oil over medium-high heat. Add the carrots, celery, garlic, shallot, and ¼ teaspoon of the salt and cook, stirring occasionally, until the vegetables are tender and the shallot is translucent, 5 to 7 minutes.

2. Stir in the oregano, basil, and tomato paste and cook for 1 minute more, or until the herbs are fragrant.

3. Add the tomatoes, lentils, balsamic vinegar, and 1 cup water and bring the sauce to a strong simmer. Reduce the heat to medium or medium-low and continue to simmer.

4. While the sauce is simmering, heat the remaining 2 tablespoons avocado oil in large skillet over medium-high heat. Crumble the tempeh so that it resembles the texture of ground beef and add it to the pan. Add the mushrooms and the tamari and cook undisturbed for 2 minutes, or until the tempeh and mushrooms have browned slightly. Stir the tempeh and mushrooms and cook, undisturbed, for 2 minutes more. Remove from the heat and transfer the mixture to the sauce. Simmer for 30 minutes, adding more water as needed to achieve the desired consistency. Taste and season with the remaining ¼ teaspoon salt, if desired. Serve with gluten-free pasta.

Pam's One and Only Vegetarian Lasagna

If I had to choose a favorite recipe from my childhood, this lasagna would be it. My mom has been making a version of this for every special occasion, family gathering, and dinner party since I was little, and whenever she offers to cook for me now, I always ask her to make it. Her secret ingredient is putting thinly sliced potatoes between the layers in lieu of classic ricotta cheese. Here, I've taken her recipe and tweaked it with my own favorite ingredients. I've made this version for my mom a few times, and she wholeheartedly approves. The sliced shiitakes give a deep umami flavor, and the spinach makes you feel good about eating three helpings of lasagna on a random weeknight! You can swap out the veggies to make it seasonal, and once you get all the components down, it's easy to master. Perfect for a cozy night in, as a family dinner (with a little garlic bread and vegan Caesar salad on the side), or to bring to a potluck. It's hard to find a vegan and gluten-free lasagna worth its layers, and this one does not disappoint. Dare I say it's one of the best lasagnas I've ever tasted—and, yes, I know that's a bold statement!

SERVES 6 TO 8

2 (9-ounce) packages **brown-rice lasagna noodles**, such as Jovial

7 tablespoons **extra-virgin olive oil**

1 pound **shiitake mushrooms**, sliced

2 tablespoons **low-sodium tamari**

5 ounces **baby spinach**

1 teaspoon **fine sea salt**

1 (24-ounce) jar **tomato sauce**, such as Rao's Marinara

2 **russet potatoes**, peeled and sliced lengthwise into ¼-inch-thick pieces

8 ounces **cashew mozzarella** or traditional mozzarella cheese

4 ounces **vegan cheese or goat cheese**

1. Preheat the oven to 375°F.

2. Prepare the lasagna noodles according to the package instructions. To prevent sticking, remove the noodles and lay them in a single layer on clean dish towels while preparing the other ingredients.

3. In a large skillet, heat 2 tablespoons of the olive oil over medium heat. Add the mushrooms and tamari and cook, stirring occasionally, until the mushrooms' moisture has evaporated and the mixture has reduced in volume by half, 5 to 7 minutes. Stir in the spinach and season with ¼ teaspoon of the salt. Allow the spinach to wilt, about 2 minutes, and incorporate it into the mushroom and tamari mixture. Remove the pan from the heat and allow to cool.

4. To assemble the lasagna, drizzle 1 tablespoon olive oil on the bottom of a 9 × 13-inch baking dish.

5. Using a large spoon, spread a thin layer, about ¼ cup, of the tomato sauce on the bottom of the dish. Add a single layer of the lasagna noodles, cutting or overlapping the noodles as needed to fit in the pan. Spread ½ cup of the tomato sauce on the naked noodles.

Recipe continues

6. Sprinkle a third of the cooked mushrooms and spinach mixture over the tomato sauce. Shingle a third of the sliced potatoes on top and then dot with a quarter of the mozzarella cheese. Season this layer with ¼ teaspoon of salt and 1 tablespoon olive oil.

7. Repeat by adding another layer of the lasagna noodles, followed by ½ cup tomato sauce, the second third of the mushroom and spinach mixture, the second third of the potato slices, the second quarter of the cheese, ¼ teaspoon salt, and 1 tablespoon olive oil. Repeat this sequence one more time.

8. For the top layer, add the remaining lasagna noodles and top with ½ to 1 cup tomato sauce, making sure the noodles are completely covered. Dot the top of the lasagna with the remaining quarter of mozzarella cheese. Crumble the goat cheese on the top of the lasagna and drizzle with the remaining 1 tablespoon of the olive oil.

9. Cover the baking dish with a layer of parchment followed by aluminum foil. Bake the lasagna for 10 to 15 minutes. Uncover and bake for 25 to 35 minutes more, until the cheese is golden brown and bubbling. Let cool slightly to set before serving. The lasagna can be covered and stored in the refrigerator for up to 5 days. If freezing, cover and store in the freezer for up to 3 months.

pasta
tomatoes
baking
jovial
Sunfood

Grains & Legumes

Golden Rice

WITH GHEE, TURMERIC, AND ONION

Ghee, a traditional ingredient in Ayurvedic cooking, is lactose-free, high in essential fatty acids, and very soothing to the gut. It's an ingredient I always keep on hand. I *love* this rice; I go to bed thinking about it and then wait excitedly for dinner on days I know I am making it. There's something so wonderful about the silky ghee, slightly bitter turmeric, and sweet, sautéed onion that just really elevates a bowl of white rice. This rice is anti-inflammatory and healing from the ghee and turmeric, and if anyone in our house is under the weather, I make a big pot of this. Sometimes if I want something more soupy, I make a miso broth and then stir in this golden rice. I think of it as a vegetarian version of a hot bowl of chicken and rice soup.

SERVES 4 TO 6

2 tablespoons ghee

1 small **yellow onion**, minced

1 (1-inch) piece **fresh ginger**, peeled

1 teaspoon **ground turmeric**

½ teaspoon **fine sea salt**

2 cups **uncooked basmati rice**, soaked in water overnight, drained, and rinsed

1. In a medium saucepan, melt the ghee over medium heat. Add the onion and cook, stirring occasionally, until translucent, 4 to 5 minutes. Grate the ginger on a Microplane and add it to the onion. Stir in the turmeric and salt and cook until the ginger is fragrant, about 1 minute more.

2. Add the rice and stir, then cook for about 1 minute to toast the rice. Add 4 cups water and bring the mixture to a boil. Reduce the heat to low, cover, and cook until the water has been fully absorbed, about 10 minutes.

3. Remove the pan from the heat and allow the rice to steam, covered, for 10 minutes. Fluff with a fork and serve warm. The rice can be stored in an airtight container in the refrigerator for up to 3 days.

No-Fail Stovetop Rice

One of the questions I get asked most on Instagram is how to cook basic rice to use for meals throughout the week. My mom has been using this method on all grains since I was a kid, and she passed it down to me. The secret to perfectly cooked rice is to turn off the heat when it's just cooked and then let it steam for an additional ten minutes, sitting covered on the stovetop. The steaming ensures that the grains are evenly cooked and fluffy and that they don't stick to the bottom of the pan and burn. I soak all my grains overnight, which breaks down the phytic acid and makes them easier to digest; you can skip this step and still wind up with perfectly cooked rice, but soaking it also speeds up the cooking time, which is helpful on weeknights. There are many nights that I don't feel like cooking anything elaborate, and I'll make a pot of this quick rice, heat up a jar of beans with a few spices, and slice some raw vegetables; it's a relaxed vegetarian meal that always hits the spot.

MAKES 3 CUPS

1 cup uncooked **jasmine rice**

Cold filtered **water**

Fine sea salt

1. Place the rice in a large bowl with cold filtered water to cover and soak overnight. Drain and rinse the rice until the water runs clear.

2. Transfer the rice to a medium high-sided pot and add 1½ cups water. Bring the water to a boil over medium-high heat. Reduce the heat to low, cover, and cook the rice for 10 minutes. Remove the pot from the heat and allow the rice to steam, covered, for 10 minutes. Fluff with a fork and season with salt to taste. The rice can be stored in an airtight container in the refrigerator for up to 3 days.

Marinated Ginger and Lime Tempeh

Tempeh is a fermented form of soy and an excellent source of gut-healthy plant protein. It beautifully absorbs flavor, so a great marinade is key. This dish is tender, juicy, and bursting with bright flavor from the lime and ginger. The trick is to not overcook the tempeh, stopping just when it is lightly browned. My family loves this as a taco filling, but you could easily cut it lengthwise into slices, sauté it, and add it to any salad or rice dish for a heartier meal. It is also delicious in burrito bowls that we make the next day with leftovers.

SERVES 4 TO 6

2 tablespoons **avocado oil**

1 pound **tempeh**, such as Lightlife Tempeh

3 **garlic cloves**, minced

1 tablespoon minced peeled **fresh ginger**

1 tablespoon low-sodium **tamari**

2 teaspoons **smoked paprika**

Zest and juice of 1 **lime**

½ teaspoon **Himalayan pink salt**

1. In a large skillet, heat the oil over medium heat. Add the tempeh and cook, breaking it up with the back of a wooden spoon, until evenly browned, about 5 minutes.

2. Stir in the garlic and ginger and cook, stirring continuously, until fragrant, 1 minute. Add the tamari, paprika, lime zest, and lime juice. Stir to combine and season with the salt. If needed, add a tablespoon of water at a time and stir to scrape up the browned bits from the bottom of the pan. Remove from the heat and serve immediately or let cool, then cover and store in the refrigerator for up to 3 days.

Coconut Tomato Rice

This rccipc came about by accident. I had extra coconut rice left over in the fridge one day and I wanted to repurpose it for Taco Tuesday. My kids love the red tomato rice that we often order in Mexican restaurants, so I decided to make an at-home version. It is perfectly creamy and coconutty, and the tomato brings acidity and a beautiful pop of color. If I'm making it for a group of adults, I add some minced jalapeños or other chiles to make it more traditional and to kick up the spice level.

MAKES 10 CUPS

1 tablespoon **coconut oil**

1 large **white onion**, chopped

1 large **tomato**, chopped

½ teaspoon **fine sea salt**

2 cups uncooked **basmati or jasmine rice**, soaked in filtered water overnight, drained, and rinsed

2 cups full-fat **coconut milk**

1. In a large high-sided pan or Dutch oven, melt the coconut oil over medium-high heat. Add the onion, tomato, and ½ teaspoon of the salt and cook until the onion is slightly translucent, 4 to 5 minutes.

2. Stir in the rice, coconut milk, and 2 cups water and bring the mixture to a simmer over medium-high heat. Reduce the heat to medium-low, cover, and cook until the liquid has been absorbed and the rice is tender but not mushy, about 15 minutes. Remove from the heat and allow the rice to steam, covered, for 10 minutes. Fluff the rice before serving. The rice can be stored in an airtight container in the refrigerator for up to 3 days.

Mexican-Style Black Beans

I could live on rice and beans. My oldest son takes after me and has loved black beans since he started solids. I'm constantly coming up with new and delicious ways to prepare them. This is my take on classic Mexican restaurant-style whole black beans. I serve them on Taco Tuesdays, as leftovers in salads, or as an after-school snack. Storing them in their cooking liquid ensures that they stay tender and flavorful. If you don't have time to make your own beans in a pressure cooker, you can absolutely use jarred or canned beans. If you prefer a refried bean consistency, puree some of these beans and veggies in a food processor or blender.

MAKES 4 CUPS

1 tablespoon **avocado oil**

1 **red bell pepper**, diced

1 **orange bell pepper**, diced

1 small **red onion**, diced

1½ cups **cooked black beans,** or 1 (15-ounce) can black beans, drained and rinsed (see Note)

½ teaspoon **fine sea salt**

1. In a large skillet, heat the avocado oil over medium heat. Add the red and orange bell peppers and onion to the pan and cook, stirring occasionally, until the onion is translucent, 5 to 7 minutes.
2. Stir in the beans and cook until heated thoroughly, 2 to 3 minutes. Taste and season with the salt. Serve, or let cool, then store in an airtight container in the refrigerator for up to 3 days.

NOTE: To make 1½ cups cooked black beans, place ½ cup dried beans in a bowl with filtered cold water to cover and soak overnight. Drain, then transfer the drained beans to a saucepan and cover with several inches of fresh water. Bring the water to a simmer and cook until the beans are tender, about 45 minutes.

“Refried” Pinto Beans

After you make this recipe, you’ll never buy another can of refried beans again. These are silky smooth and so flavorful and delicious—they really taste like the real deal. I keep them simple with just a little sautéed onion and avocado oil, but you can easily add in paprika, cumin, and other spices or even a little toasted garlic. These are a great way to introduce young kids to beans, and all my boys enjoyed them when they were first starting solids. My middle son has been on a whole-bean strike for a few years, but he happily devours these in tacos and quesadillas.

MAKES 3 CUPS

2 tablespoons **avocado oil**

1 small **yellow onion**, chopped

½ teaspoon **fine sea salt**

2 (15-ounce) cans **pinto beans**, drained and rinsed, or 2 cups **Basic Pressure Cooker Beans** (page 202)

1. In a large skillet, heat the avocado oil over medium heat. Add the onion and salt and cook, stirring occasionally, until slightly softened, 2 to 3 minutes. Stir in the beans and cook, stirring occasionally, until the beans are softened and warmed through, 2 to 3 minutes. Remove from the heat and allow the beans to cool slightly.

2. Add the beans to a high-speed blender or food processor. Pulse, adding ¼ cup water at a time until the mixture has the texture and thickness of hummus, about ½ cup water total. The refried beans can be covered and stored in the refrigerator for up to 3 days.

Baked Polenta

WITH MARINARA AND SOFT GOAT CHEESE

This is a standout entrée when you want to wow a crowd with a meatless meal. I have never loved soft, creamy polenta, but baked polenta, which turns golden brown and firm once chilled and baked, is delicious! If your pantry is well stocked, you can whip this up on a whim. I always rely on my favorite jar of marinara and make sure to have fine-ground polenta on hand. I love to serve this with garlicky sautéed kale and garlic bread for a hearty Italian feast. Sometimes I will heat up a jar of cannellini beans in the marinara and pour it over the baked polenta; the beans add a little bit of extra protein and fiber and really turn this into a complete meal. It makes a beautiful addition to any dinner spread, so I often serve this when entertaining guests.

SERVES 4 TO 6

1 cup **fine-ground polenta**

1 teaspoon **fine sea salt**

2 tablespoons **unsalted butter** (optional)

1¼ cups **Slow-Roasted Chunky Tomato Sauce** (page 42) or store-bought marinara

4 ounces **goat cheese**, crumbled

1. In a large pot or Dutch oven, bring 8 cups water to a boil over medium-high heat. Reduce the heat to medium-low and slowly whisk in the polenta. Cook, whisking frequently, until the polenta begins to thicken, 50 to 60 minutes. Season with the salt and butter, if desired.

2. Pour the polenta into a large baking dish or 7 × 9-inch baking pan and allow it to cool and set completely, at least one hour. (You can refrigerate it to expedite this process.)

3. Preheat the broiler to high.

4. Evenly spread the tomato sauce over the cooled polenta and dot the top of the dish with the goat cheese. Broil the polenta for 2 to 3 minutes, until the goat cheese is lightly browned and the sauce is bubbling. Serve warm.

Basic Pressure Cooker Beans

Sure, you can always buy canned or jarred beans, and I absolutely recommend keeping a few of those in your pantry for emergency meal situations, but the best way to consume beans for both flavor and digestion is to soak them and cook them yourself! Since the mainstay of our diet is whole, vegetable-focused foods, I rely on protein-packed vegetarian staples to throw meals together whenever I need to. I keep a container of these stewed beans in the refrigerator and toss them into salads or a marinara sauce, or grain bowls and, of course, into tacos, quesadillas, and nachos. Investing in an Instant Pot was worth it for the ability to make my own beans a few times a week, and because these are so easy to digest, the whole family benefits from them. Don't be afraid to add in any extras like veggie scraps, garlic, and onions or anything else you have lying around that might add flavor and depth to the bean broth. And don't toss that broth—I freeze it and then use it to boost soups and stews, as you would with a meat or vegetable broth.

MAKES 3 CUPS

1 cup **dried beans**, soaked overnight in water, then drained

2 **garlic cloves**, peeled

1 piece **dried kombu**

Fill an Instant Pot or pressure cooker with 8 cups water. Add the beans, garlic, and kombu. Seal the lid, then cook on high pressure for 30 minutes. Release the pressure, allowing it to escape naturally. Cool completely and store in an airtight container in the refrigerator for up to 3 days.

Coco Rice

The best coconut rice I've ever tasted was during a surf trip in a tiny restaurant tucked away on my favorite tropical island. It was creamy but not mushy, just perfectly sweet and topped with toasted coconut flakes. Absolute heaven, though maybe I thought so because gorgeous waves were breaking just ten feet in front of me. But I've tried a lot of coconut rice and that one always wins. I've spent a long time perfecting my own coconut rice. I choose to omit the coconut sugar and instead let the natural sweetness of full-fat coconut milk and coconut flakes take center stage. I think this recipe is as delicious as the original that inspired it, and I'm usually standing in my apartment in a concrete jungle when I'm eating it. But every bite transports me back to paradise—just don't ask me where because that's a secret and I won't spill the beans, or the rice.

MAKES 3 CUPS

1 cup uncooked **jasmine rice**, soaked in filtered water overnight, drained, and rinsed

1¾ cups full-fat **coconut milk**

½ teaspoon fine **sea salt**

½ cup unsweetened **coconut flakes**, toasted

1. In a medium saucepan, combine the rice, coconut milk, and ¼ cup water. Bring the mixture to a boil over medium-high heat. Reduce the heat to low, cover, and cook for 10 minutes. Remove the pan from the heat and allow the rice to steam, covered, for 10 minutes. Fluff with a fork and season with the salt.

2. Garnish the rice with the toasted coconut flakes and serve. The rice can be stored in an airtight container in the refrigerator for up to 3 days.

Kasha

WITH CARAMELIZED ONIONS AND CRISPY SHIITAKES

One of my goals with this cookbook is to encourage you to try foods outside of your comfort zone—foods that are quick to prepare, delicious, and nutrient-dense. Never heard of kasha? It's a grain traditionally used in Eastern European dishes, and it's an excellent alternative to rice or quinoa. Kasha is made from buckwheat groats and is naturally gluten-free. The kernels don't look like much at the grocery store, but they transform into a delicious fluffy pilaf once cooked. This was one of my mom's staple recipes when I was growing up. The very thinly sliced sweet onions and the crispy umami shiitakes balance out the earthiness of the cooked kasha. It's a wonderful base for a grain bowl, or great as a side dish with your cozy favorite soup.

SERVES 4 TO 6

6 tablespoons **avocado oil**

2 **shallots**, sliced

2 **garlic cloves**, coarsely chopped

½ teaspoon **fine sea salt**

½ pound **shiitake mushrooms**, thinly sliced

2 tablespoons **low-sodium tamari**

1 cup **kasha**

1. In a large pan, heat 3 tablespoons of the avocado oil over medium heat. Add the shallots and cook, stirring occasionally, until golden brown, 8 to 10 minutes. Add the garlic and ¼ teaspoon of the salt, and cook, stirring occasionally, until the garlic is fragrant, about 1 minute.

2. Increase the heat to medium-high and add the remaining 3 tablespoons avocado oil. Add the mushrooms and cook, undisturbed, for 2 minutes. Stir the shallots and shiitakes together and cook, undisturbed, for 2 minutes more. Reduce the heat to low to keep the mixture warm while you prepare the kasha.

3. In a saucepan, combine the kasha and 2 cups water. Bring the water to a simmer over medium-high heat and cook, stirring occasionally, until the kasha has absorbed the water and is tender, 2 to 3 minutes.

4. Add the caramelized shallots, crispy shiitakes, and tamari to the kasha, season with the remaining ¼ teaspoon salt, and stir to combine. Serve immediately, or let cool, then cover and store in the refrigerator for up to 3 days.

Buttery Short Grain Brown Rice

WITH CRISPY BRUSSELS SPROUTS AND SHALLOTS

Here's a statement that might come as a surprise to everyone: I like white rice better than brown rice. I know that seems counterintuitive in a healthy foods book, but I'm all about keeping it real. The one exception to this preference is nutty, buttery short-grain brown rice, which is about as perfect as a grain can get. I've added crispy Brussels sprouts (which is really the only way to enjoy a Brussels sprout) and sautéed shallots that caramelize as they cook in the sizzling butter. The finished product is a silky, pillowy but sturdy rice dish that is perfect for cooking at the beginning of a busy week and then enjoying throughout. If you want to make a smaller portion, simply cut the recipe in half. While this recipe does have a few steps, each can be done simultaneously, leaving you free to make the rest of your meal while the Brussels sprouts roast and the rice cooks. If you aren't a Brussels sprouts fan, you can sub broccoli or even roasted button mushrooms. I love to serve this with a big, bright salad and maple and coconut roasted kabocha squash for a perfect fall meal.

SERVES 6 TO 8

3 tablespoons **unsalted butter**

3 large **shallots**, thinly sliced

2 teaspoons **fine sea salt**, plus more if needed

2 pounds **Brussels sprouts**, trimmed and quartered

3 tablespoons **extra-virgin olive oil**

3 cups uncooked **short-grain brown rice**, soaked in filtered water overnight, drained, and rinsed

Juice of 2 **lemons**

1. Preheat the oven to 425°F.

2. In a large skillet, melt the butter over medium heat. Add the shallots and ½ teaspoon of the salt and cook, stirring occasionally and reducing the heat as needed to prevent too much browning, until the shallots are lightly caramelized, 20 to 25 minutes. Remove from the heat.

3. Divide the Brussels sprouts between two baking sheets. Season each sheet with 1 tablespoon of the olive oil and ½ teaspoon salt. Roast the Brussels sprouts until tender and crispy, 15 to 20 minutes. Remove from the oven.

4. Meanwhile, in a large Dutch oven, combine the rice, remaining ½ teaspoon salt, and 6 cups water. Bring the mixture to a boil over medium-high heat. Reduce the heat to low, cover, and cook, until the liquid has been fully absorbed, 20 to 25 minutes. Remove from the heat and fluff the rice with a fork.

5. Add the buttery shallots, crispy Brussels sprouts, lemon juice, and remaining 1 tablespoon olive oil to the rice. Stir to fully combine and taste for seasoning. Serve immediately, or let cool, then cover and store in the refrigerator for up to 3 days.

Soups & Stews

Gingery Butternut Squash Soup

I probably eat a bowl of this soup every day when butternut squash is in season. I cannot get enough of it. It's luxurious and decadent but quick and simple to prepare, and it's filled with antioxidants. The rich golden-orange color is stunning. I don't love sweet soup, so I add extra ginger to cut the sweetness of the squash. Roasting the squash means that it gets a little caramelized with all the herbs and just takes this up a notch from if you were to simply steam or sauté the squash in the pot before pureeing. I love to ladle this over bowls of Coco Rice (page 203)—perfection!

SERVES 4

1 **butternut squash**, peeled and cut into 1-inch pieces

1 small **yellow onion**, diced

1 tablespoon **extra-virgin avocado oil**

¾ teaspoon **fine sea salt**

Leaves from 3 to 4 **thyme sprigs**

1 (1-inch) piece **fresh ginger**, peeled

Toasted coconut flakes, for garnish (optional)

1. Preheat the oven to 350°F. Line a baking sheet with parchment paper.
2. Place the butternut squash and onion on the prepared baking sheet and season with the avocado oil, ½ teaspoon of the salt, and the thyme. Bake for 40 minutes, or until tender when poked with a paring knife or fork. Remove from the oven and allow to cool slightly.
3. Working in batches, transfer about half the baked squash and onion to a high-speed blender or food processor. Grate the ginger over the vegetables. Carefully blend the mixture, adding 1 cup water as you blend, until the soup is pureed and silky in texture. Pour the pureed soup into a large pot and repeat with the remaining vegetables, adding up to 1½ cups water to the blender. (Alternatively, transfer the vegetables to a large pot, grate in the ginger, and use an immersion blender to blend the soup directly in the pot, adding up to 2½ cups water as you blend.)
4. Bring the soup to a simmer over low heat. Taste and season with the remaining ¼ teaspoon salt, if needed.
5. Divide the soup evenly among four bowls, garnish with toasted coconut flakes, if desired, and serve.

Navy Beans and Greens Soup

This soup brings me infinite comfort. It's easy to throw together without being bland, and you can swap in any kind of white bean you like. I love navy beans because they are small and delicate, and even non-bean eaters tend to enjoy them. I'd bet that on days you're low on groceries, you still have the ingredients for this soup in your fridge. I prefer to soak dry beans overnight and pressure-cook them (see page 202), but you can just as successfully use jarred beans (or canned, in a pinch) for this soup. Jovial makes great jarred cannellini beans, which work well in place of the navy beans. I frequently eat a bowl of this as a midday snack or with a salad and some leftover quinoa or brown rice for lunch, or with toasty bread for dinner. You can even sprinkle a little goat cheese on top and add a few toasted croutons, if you want to make it a little more Tuscan. Tossing in the greens at the last minute ensures that they stay vibrant and full of nutrients.

SERVES 6 TO 8

¼ cup **avocado oil**

1 small **yellow onion**, diced

2 **garlic cloves**, chopped

6 **celery stalks**, chopped

3 **carrots**, chopped

1 **russet potato**, unpeeled, chopped

¾ teaspoon **fine sea salt**

1 tablespoon **garlic powder**

1 tablespoon **onion powder**

1 teaspoon **dried thyme**

1 teaspoon **dried oregano**

½ cup **dried navy beans** soaked overnight and cooked, or 1 (15-ounce) can navy beans, drained and rinsed

1 bunch **kale**, stems removed and leaves chopped

¼ cup chopped **fresh cilantro**, for garnish (optional)

Extra-virgin olive oil, for garnish (optional)

1. In a large pot or Dutch oven, heat the avocado oil over medium-high heat. Add the onion and cook, stirring occasionally, until slightly softened, 2 to 3 minutes. Stir in the garlic and cook until fragrant, 1 minute.

2. Add the celery, carrots, potato, and ½ teaspoon of the salt. Cook the vegetables, stirring occasionally, until the vegetables are soft and tender but retain their color, 5 to 7 minutes. Add 1 to 2 tablespoons of water to deglaze the pan, as needed. Stir in the garlic powder, onion powder, thyme, and oregano.

3. Add the beans and 4 to 6 cups of water, or enough to cover the beans and the vegetables. Bring the mixture to a boil and then reduce the heat to medium-low and simmer for 30 minutes. The liquid should be slightly reduced and thickened, and the beans and vegetables should be tender but intact. Stir in the kale and season with the remaining ¼ teaspoon salt.

4. To serve, ladle into bowls while warm and, if desired, garnish with the fresh cilantro and a drizzle of olive oil.

Chilly Day Chili

WITH ALL THE TOPPINGS

I will admit it's taken me years to like chili, even though I've always wanted to. One issue is I don't love kidney beans, which are usually front and center in chili, and honestly, it just gives me heartburn a few minutes after I eat it. We spend a lot of time in the mountains, where chili is very popular, so I got to work perfecting this recipe, and now I am a convert. This is a veggie-forward version. I use a mix of black and pinto beans and omit the usual corn, which, in my opinion, usually adds to post-chili indigestion. You can adjust the spice level by upping or lowering the amount of cayenne pepper and garnishing with a few fresh jalapeños at the end. I like to make a chili bar and place all the fixings and toppings on the counter, and then let the kids top their own. Spoiler alert: Mine always choose extra shredded cheese and dairy-free sour cream. They lick the bowls clean and usually ask for seconds.

SERVES 4 TO 6

2 tablespoons **avocado oil**

2 **celery stalks**, chopped

1 small **yellow onion**, chopped

1 **yellow bell pepper**, chopped

1 **green bell pepper**, chopped

2 **garlic cloves**, chopped

¾ teaspoon **fine sea salt**

½ teaspoon **smoked paprika**

½ teaspoon **dried cumin**

⅛ teaspoon **cayenne**

2 tablespoons **tomato paste**

1 (13-ounce) jar **pinto beans**, such as Jovial, or 1 (15-ounce) can, drained and rinsed

1 (13-ounce) jar **black beans**, such as Jovial, or 1 (15-ounce) can, drained and rinsed

1 (15-ounce) can **crushed tomatoes**

For Serving

Shredded **goat cheese**

Sliced **jalapeños**

Dairy-free sour cream

Diced **avocado**

1. In a large Dutch oven, heat the avocado oil over medium-high heat. Add the celery, onion, yellow and green bell peppers, garlic, and ¼ teaspoon of the salt. Cook, stirring occasionally, until the vegetables are tender but still retain their bright colors, 5 to 7 minutes.

2. Stir in the paprika, cumin, cayenne, and tomato paste and cook for 1 minute to toast the spices and tomato paste. Add the pinto beans, black beans, remaining ½ teaspoon salt, crushed tomatoes, and 1½ cups water. Bring the mixture to a strong simmer, then reduce the heat to medium-low and simmer gently for about 1 hour.

3. Divide the chili among bowls and serve with goat cheese, jalapeños, sour cream, and avocado on the table so everyone can top their chili as they like.

Spicy Lentil Stew

WITH TOMATO AND WILTED GREENS

Lentils are the most versatile legume and are a key staple in my recipe wheelhouse. They are the perfect size and texture, loaded with essential nutrients and minerals, and very easy to digest. There are many popular stew recipes using red lentils, and they are delicious, but I love to use green or brown lentils for this dish. Cooking down the whole fresh tomatoes gives it more of a rustic farmhouse vibe, but if you are short on time or tomatoes, a jar of pasta sauce or canned whole tomatoes will work just fine. I love to cook with Calabrian chiles and always try to have a jar in the pantry, but if you can't find them, use red pepper flakes for a similar effect. Any green works here, but the spinach holds up well, which means delicious leftovers *and* healthy meals with minimal mess and cleanup during the week. This is a great stew to repurpose: Throw it over pasta one night, or put the leftovers in a casserole dish and bake with some vegan cheese or goat cheese on top until melted and bubbling, and then serve it over rice or buttery toast.

SERVES 4 TO 6

3 tablespoons **extra-virgin olive oil**

3 to 4 large **beefsteak tomatoes**, chopped

2 **garlic cloves**, coarsely chopped

¾ teaspoon **fine sea salt**

1 teaspoon **tomato paste**

1 teaspoon **Calabrian chile paste**

2 cups cooked **green lentils**

4 cups **baby spinach**

2 cups cooked **brown rice** or 4 cups cooked penne, for serving (optional)

1. In a large Dutch oven, heat the olive oil over medium-high heat. Add the tomatoes, garlic, and ½ teaspoon of the salt and cook, stirring occasionally, until the garlic is fragrant and the tomatoes begin to become jammy, 2 to 3 minutes. Stir in the tomato paste and cook for 2 minutes more, or until the mixture thickens slightly.

2. Add the chile paste, lentils, and ¼ cup of water and bring the mixture to a simmer. Season with the remaining ¼ teaspoon salt and stir in the spinach. Reduce the heat to medium-low and cook, stirring occasionally, until the spinach has wilted and fully incorporated with the tomatoes and lentils, about 2 minutes. Remove from the heat and serve hot.

Ginger Vegetable Miso Soup

When you're in need of something healing and incredibly delicious, this is the soup for you! Miso is so healthy and nutrient-dense, and because it is fermented, it's great for the gut. This is my version of chicken noodle soup. I love this extra-brothy version with tender shiitakes, carrots, and Asian greens. The freshly grated ginger is an immune-boosting powerhouse. Once you master this version, feel free to make it your own: You could add hijiki or wakame seaweed, ramen noodles, or even cubes of tofu. Make sure to remove the broth from the heat before you add your miso paste to it—miso is a living culture, and exposure to high heat kills all the good bacteria that you want to reap the benefits from, especially when you're under the weather!

SERVES 6 TO 8

2 tablespoons **avocado oil**

3 **carrots**, cut into matchsticks

1 small **yellow onion**, sliced

1 **Yukon Gold potato**, cut into matchsticks

4 teaspoons **fine sea salt**, plus more if needed

3 to 4 ounces **shiitake mushrooms**, sliced (about 1 cup)

2 cups thinly sliced **napa cabbage**

1 cup **frozen edamame**, defrosted

4 heads **baby bok choy**, chopped (about 4 cups)

¼ cup **white miso paste**

1 (1-inch) piece **fresh ginger**, peeled

1. In a large stockpot, heat the avocado oil over medium heat. Add the carrots, onion, potato, and 2 teaspoons of the salt. Cook, stirring occasionally, until the vegetables begin to soften, 2 to 3 minutes. Add 8 cups water and bring to a simmer, then add the mushrooms, cabbage, and edamame and cook until the cabbage is tender, about 3 minutes. Season the soup with the remaining 2 teaspoons salt.

2. Remove the soup from the heat and stir in the bok choy. Set a fine-mesh strainer on the top of the soup; it should sit in the soup but not be fully submerged. Place the miso in the strainer so it's submerged and allow it to dissolve for 10 to 15 minutes as the soup cools. (This will prevent grittiness.)

3. Remove the strainer and any undissolved miso remaining in the strainer. Using a Microplane, grate the ginger into the soup. Taste the soup for seasoning and, if necessary, add up to 2 teaspoons more salt.

Sweets

Baked Apples

WITH CINNAMON AND MAPLE

This is probably the first dessert my mom taught me to make, and the smell of this dish always reminds me of cozy fall days spent coring apples in my childhood kitchen. My mom would place a stool for me to stand on and let me use a circular apple slicer. Then I'd find the cinnamon sticks from the spice drawer and measure out the maple syrup. We always added raisins or currants, and I ate as many as I placed in the baking dish. Once it was baked and golden and piping-hot, my dad would serve heaping scoops of vanilla ice cream, and we'd spoon the apples on top. The next time you go apple picking and have a basket full of apples that you don't know what to do with, make this. It's peak fall perfection.

SERVES 8

4 **Honeycrisp apples**

2 tablespoons **ghee**

2 tablespoons **pure maple syrup**

1 teaspoon **ground cinnamon**

¼ cup **coconut sugar**

1. Preheat the oven to 375°F.

2. Cut ¼ inch from the bottom of each apple so that they sit upright. Using an apple corer, a tablespoon, or a paring knife, create a 2- to 3-tablespoon cavity in the top of each apple; do not cut all the way through to the bottom. Discard any excess interior apple flesh. Stand the apples upright in a 7×9-inch or similar-size baking dish.

3. In a small saucepan, melt the ghee over low heat. Whisk in the maple syrup and cinnamon and pour it evenly over the apples. Sprinkle the apples with the coconut sugar and bake until the apples are tender and the sugar is caramelized and bubbly, 50 to 55 minutes. Let cool slightly before serving. Leftovers can be covered and stored in the refrigerator for up to 3 days. To reheat, bake at 350°F for 10 to 12 minutes, until warmed through.

Vanilla Doughnuts

WITH BLUE MAGIC GLAZE

If you've followed me on Instagram for a long time, you know that one of my biggest pet peeves is artificial dyes in our food. If there's one ingredient we know to be universally bad for, and especially disruptive to, children's health, it's petroleum-based food dyes. Kids love brightly colored treats because they are constantly surrounded by them, so I'm always looking for fun ways to use plant-based colors. My mom has been using spirulina and butterfly pea flower powder since I was little, but I had never thought to use it for a cake glaze until I saw a wonderful bakery in upstate New York share their vibrantly colored gluten-free doughnuts. My boys are obsessed with doughnuts, so I surprised them with these one weekend and got rave reviews. These are baked in molds instead of fried, so the base is more similar to cake than a traditional doughnut, making them a wonderful naturally sweetened dessert to enjoy any day of the week.

MAKES 12 DOUGHNUTS

1 cup **gluten-free all-purpose flour** without xanthan gum, such as Bob's Red Mill

1 cup **almond flour**

⅔ cup **coconut sugar**

2½ teaspoons **baking powder**

¼ teaspoon **baking soda**

½ teaspoon **fine sea salt**

1 teaspoon **ground cinnamon**

1 cup unsweetened **oat milk**

½ cup **coconut oil**, melted

2 large **eggs**

¾ cup **powdered maple sugar**

¼ teaspoon **blue butterfly pea flower powder**

1. Preheat the oven to 350°F.

2. In a large bowl, whisk together the all-purpose flour, almond flour, coconut sugar, baking powder, baking soda, salt, cinnamon, oat milk, coconut oil, and eggs until smooth and free of lumps.

3. Using a nonstick doughnut baking tray, spoon ¼ cup of the batter into each doughnut mold. Bake for 15 minutes, or until the doughnuts are dry, golden brown, and pull away from the sides of the pan. Allow them to cool slightly, then remove them from the pan and let cool completely, about 10 minutes.

4. Meanwhile, in a small bowl, whisk together the powdered maple sugar and 2 tablespoons water. In another small bowl, whisk together the blue butterfly pea flower powder and ½ teaspoon water. Add a few drops of the blue to the maple sugar and, using a spoon, gently swirl the two together to create the look of tie-dye. Do not overstir the icing unless you'd prefer a solid blue color.

5. To ice the doughnuts, dip the top into the icing, then let any excess icing drip off before flipping the doughnut over and placing it on a plate to set. Repeat for each doughnut.

6. Serve immediately or store in an airtight container at room temperature for up to 3 days.

No-Bake Peanut Butter Granola Bars

WITH CHOCOLATE DRIZZLE

These are quick no-bake treats that are sinfully delicious and packed with great ingredients. They are sweetened only with dates and a touch of raw honey, so I feel good about bringing these to school pickup or sports practice for a sweet treat. Because the ingredients are so pure, these won't hold up like a typical processed bar. It's best to keep them chilled until you're ready to snack on one (but they'll hold up fine if you're taking them with you as a snack on the go). If you want to experiment with different superfood ingredients like chia seeds or goji berries, feel free to throw them in; the batter is forgiving, and if the oat-date ratio is precise, other additions will work well. I use pecans and pumpkin seeds because those are our favorites, but cashews or almonds would work well too, cup for cup. This is the kind of sweet that reminds you just how delicious better-for-you homemade treats and snacks can be.

MAKES 12 BARS

6 pitted **Medjool dates**

2 tablespoons **raw honey**

⅓ cup plus 1 tablespoon creamy **peanut butter**

1 cup **rolled oats**

1 cup **pecans**

1 cup hulled raw **pumpkin seeds**

2 tablespoons **coconut oil**

½ cup **semisweet chocolate chips**

Maldon **flaky sea salt**, for garnish (optional)

1. Line a baking sheet with parchment paper.

2. In a food processor, place the dates, honey, peanut butter, oats, pecans, pumpkin seeds, and coconut oil. Pulse until the nuts are broken down to the size of lentils, then process until the mixture resembles a dough, 2 to 3 minutes.

3. Remove the dough and press evenly into the prepared baking sheet.

4. Place the chocolate chips in a double boiler or in a heatproof bowl sitting over a pot of boiling water (make sure the bottom of the bowl doesn't touch the water). Stir the chips until the chocolate is melted. Cool slightly and drizzle over the granola mixture. Place in the refrigerator to set for at least 45 minutes. Before serving, sprinkle with flaky sea salt, if desired, and cut into squares. Store in an airtight container for up to 5 days.

Spring Café Aspen Vegan and Gluten-Free Chocolate Chip Cookies

I would bet that there are a bunch of you who bought this book just for this never-before-shared recipe. We've gone through hundreds of iterations of these cookies before coming up with this beloved version. I am a chocolate chip cookie devotee, and I have very specific requirements. Chewy, crisp edges, molten slightly underbaked center, tons of chocolate chips, and a perfectly golden brown exterior. I don't want to admit how many of these I ate while we were recipe testing, and when they first come out of the Café ovens all warm and gooey, forget about it! I wish I could tell you exactly how we stumbled upon this cookie, but the truth is it was a labor of love for me and all the wonderful chefs and bakers who have passed through the doors of Spring Café Aspen. If you've been waiting for this recipe, I'm very happy to finally share it, and I hope we will still see you for an afternoon cookie and turmeric latte in Aspen or New York City.

MAKES 13 LARGE COOKIES

3 cups **almond flour**

3 cups **gluten-free all-purpose flour**

2 teaspoons **baking soda**

1 teaspoon **fine sea salt**

1 tablespoon plus 2 teaspoons **powder egg replacer**, such as Bob's Red Mill Egg Replacer

½ cup (1 stick) **vegan butter**, melted and cooled

⅓ cup **pure maple syrup**

¼ cup full-fat **coconut milk**

2 teaspoons **pure vanilla extract**

1½ to 2 cups **vegan dark chocolate chips**

1. Preheat the oven to 325°F. Line two baking sheets with parchment paper.

2. In the bowl of a stand mixer fitted with the paddle attachment, or in a large bowl using a whisk or handheld mixer, combine the almond flour, gluten-free flour, baking soda, salt, and egg replacer and beat on low speed until fully combined and no flour clumps remain, about 1 minute.

3. In a medium bowl, whisk together the melted butter, maple syrup, coconut milk, vanilla, and 2 tablespoons cold water.

4. With the mixer on low speed, slowly add the wet ingredients and mix until everything is fully combined and the batter has the consistency of cookie dough, about 3 minutes. (If mixing by hand, switch to a large rubber spatula and slowly incorporate the wet ingredients into the dry ingredients until fully combined and the batter has the consistency of cookie dough.) Fold in the chocolate chips. Refrigerate the cookie dough for at least 1 hour or up to 4 hours.

5. Form the chilled dough into 13 equal-size balls (about 112 grams each). Shape each ball of dough as you would a veggie burger patty, about 1 inch thick and 4 inches in diameter. Place the cookies on the prepared baking sheets, spacing them evenly; they will not spread. Bake for 16 to 18 minutes, until dry and just golden. Store in an airtight container for up to 5 days.

Zucchini Banana Snacking Bread

One summer a few years ago, my zucchini plant was a serious overachiever. I'm talking more zucchini than even a zucchini lover could know what to do with. My zucchini plant was like the magic pasta pot in *Strega Nona* that Big Anthony doesn't know how to turn off. Try as I might to convince my children, they would not eat zucchini after the age of two. I'm not sure what happens, but it's like some kind of anti-zucchini biological clock in their body goes off and they suddenly decide it's gross. I had all this zucchini and nothing to do with it, so I decided to put it in a dessert. My kids love banana bread as much as they hate zucchini, and they also love to snack on baked goods, which means I like to make things that are nutrient-dense and not too sweet. This recipe took multiple tries before they would accept it as delicious, but when I finally hit the loaf on the head, they devoured it in one afternoon. The best part is the topping of hemp seeds and coconut sugar, which gives the bread a little crunch. Now my kids get excited whenever the zucchini plant goes into overdrive because they know it means this snacking bread is coming. Asked if they'll eat zucchini any other way, the answer is still no, but that doesn't stop me from trying.

MAKES 1 LOAF

1 teaspoon **coconut oil**, melted

1 large **zucchini**

1½ cups **oat flour**

½ cup **brown rice flour**

¼ cup **coconut sugar**, plus more if making the topping

1 tablespoon **baking powder**

2 ripe **bananas**, peeled

2 large **eggs**

½ cup **oat milk**

½ cup unsweetened **coconut yogurt**

¼ cup **pure maple syrup**

1 teaspoon **pure vanilla extract**

3 tablespoons **hemp seeds**, for garnish (optional)

1. Preheat the oven to 350°F. Grease a 8½ × 4½-inch loaf pan with the melted coconut oil and line it with parchment paper, leaving about 1 inch of parchment overhanging the longer sides of the pan.

2. Place a box grater over a clean, dry kitchen towel. Grate the zucchini on the large holes of the grater, then gather the grated zucchini in the towel and twist the top to squeeze out as much moisture as possible.

3. In a large bowl, whisk together the oat flour, brown rice flour, coconut sugar, and baking powder. Using your hands or a fork, mash the bananas and add them to the dry ingredients. Add the grated zucchini, eggs, oat milk, yogurt, maple syrup, and vanilla and whisk until the batter is fully combined. Pour the batter into the prepared loaf pan and sprinkle the top with some coconut sugar and the hemp seeds, if desired.

4. Bake for 60 to 70 minutes, until the top is dry and golden brown and a toothpick inserted into the center comes out with only a few moist crumbs attached. Allow the snacking bread to cool slightly (this will prevent the center from sinking in), then use the overhanging parchment to remove it from the pan. Allow it to cool completely before slicing and serving. Store in an airtight container for up to 5 days.

A Very Good Crumble

Everyone should have one dessert in their arsenal that never fails them. This crumble is mine. I am not a baker; however, I do love to serve a homemade dessert. It's not that I don't aspire to bake, I do, but try as I might to follow a recipe, I inevitably stray, making substitutions, opening the oven one too many times, and generally ending up with something other than a perfect finished product. If you're looking for a simple recipe with lots of room for error, this crumble is for you. If the topping starts to brown too heavily before the fruit starts to bubble, remove it from the oven and cover it with a layer of parchment and aluminum foil and then put it back in the oven. You can make this a few hours ahead of time and then reheat it when you're ready to serve. In the summer, I make the crumble with blueberries, but it's delicious in the fall with apples, a little spice, and a big scoop of vegan coconut ice cream. This recipe makes a little extra crumble dough, which I happily freeze and have on hand for any unexpected dinner guests or when my kids come home from school begging for a special treat.

SERVES 6 TO 8

1 cup **oat flour**

1 cup **rolled oats**

½ cup (1 stick) **unsalted butter or vegan butter**, cubed

½ cup **coconut sugar**

8 cups fresh **blueberries**

1 tablespoon **pure maple syrup**

Zest of 1 **lemon**

1 (1-inch) piece **fresh ginger**, peeled and grated

1 teaspoon **pure vanilla extract**

1. Preheat the oven to 375°F.

2. In a large bowl, combine the oat flour, rolled oats, butter, and coconut sugar. Using your hands or a fork, work the butter into the flour until the mixture begins to come together and resemble a dough. The crumble is ready when you can grab a handful of the mixture and it stays together. Set aside.

3. Place the blueberries in a 7 × 11-inch or similar-size baking dish. Evenly distribute the maple syrup, lemon zest, ginger, and vanilla over the blueberries, then evenly top the blueberries with the crumble. Bake for 40 to 45 minutes, until the crumble is golden brown and the blueberries are bubbling. Allow the crumble to cool slightly before serving. Store in an airtight container at room temperature for up to 2 days.

LE CREUSET

Double-Chocolate Skillet Cookie

A skillet cookie has all the best elements of a chocolate chip cookie but requires half the effort and produces a fraction of the mess. I love baking this because it is truly hard to screw up. If you don't measure the ingredients perfectly, or if you make a few pantry swaps, you will still wind up with a completely delicious, extra-chocolaty dessert. If you want more of a sliceable cookie, let it cool completely before serving. We can never wait that long and eat it straight out of the oven; it's more like molten fudge that way, and it's especially decadent with vanilla ice cream melting on top.

SERVES 4 TO 6

1 cup **oat flour**

1 cup **almond flour**

½ cup **coconut sugar**

1 teaspoon **baking powder**

½ teaspoon **baking soda**

4 tablespoons **coconut oil**, melted, plus more for the skillet

⅓ cup **pure maple syrup**

1 teaspoon **pure vanilla extract**

1 (15-ounce) can **pure pumpkin puree**

¼ cup unsweetened **cocoa powder**

1 cup **dark chocolate chips**

1. Preheat the oven to 350°F. Grease a 9-inch or similar-size ovenproof skillet with coconut oil.

2. In a large bowl, whisk together the oat flour, almond flour, coconut sugar, baking powder, and baking soda. Make a well in the center of the dry ingredients and add the coconut oil, maple syrup, vanilla, pumpkin, and cocoa powder to it. Stir until just combined, then fold in the chocolate chips. Pour the batter into the prepared skillet.

3. Bake for 25 minutes, or until the top is dry and a knife or toothpick inserted into the center of the cookie comes out clean. Allow the cookie to cool completely before cutting and serving.

Coconut Lemon Tart

WITH NUTTY SHORTBREAD CRUST

My dad is a Key lime pie aficionado and orders it for dessert any time he sees it on a menu. I share his love for it but don't consider myself an experienced enough baker to make a proper Key lime pie. It's also not a dessert that can be perfectly replicated with natural or dairy-free ingredients. I happily indulge once in a while, so I wanted a dessert with a similar flavor profile and a delicious citrus curd that I could make at home and feel good about serving to my family. This tart checks all those boxes. It's light enough that you don't feel like you've overdone it before bed, but also luxurious from the coconut cream and nutty crust. This tart does need to chill properly to achieve its maximum potential, so if you make it, be sure you have the time and patience to leave it in the refrigerator. It's so delicious that taking "one little bite" easily turns into eating the entire tart before it's even cool enough to serve.

SERVES 8 TO 10

1 cup **gluten-free graham crackers**, such as Simple Mills

¾ cup **walnuts**

¾ cup **cashews**

4 to 5 tablespoons **coconut oil**, melted, plus more for greasing and for serving

1 cup **fresh lemon juice**

¾ cup **maple sugar**

¼ cup **arrowroot powder**

1 (5.4-ounce) **can coconut cream**

¼ to ½ cup unsweetened **coconut shavings**, toasted, for garnish

1 teaspoon **lemon zest**, for garnish

1. Preheat the oven to 350°F. Grease the bottom and sides of a 9-inch springform pan (or a tart pan with a removable bottom) with coconut oil.

2. In a food processor, combine the graham crackers, walnuts, and cashews and pulse until finely ground. Add the coconut oil and pulse until the mixture pulls away from the sides of the food processor and retains its shape when squeezed together between two fingers.

3. Press the crust mixture in an even layer over the bottom of the prepared pan. Bake for about 15 minutes, until the crust is fragrant, slightly toasted, and dry. Allow the crust to cool completely, at least 30 minutes.

4. Meanwhile, in a small saucepan, heat the lemon juice and maple sugar over medium heat. In a small bowl, combine the arrowroot powder with 3 tablespoons water and set aside for 2 minutes (this "blooms" the arrowroot). Whisk the arrowroot mixture into the lemon juice mixture. Bring the mixture to a strong simmer, whisking continuously, until it is thickened, about 1 minute. It should have the texture of jam.

5. Reduce the heat to low and whisk in the coconut cream until combined. Remove the filling from the heat. If you see any lumps, pass it through a fine-mesh strainer to remove them. Allow the filling to cool until no longer warm to the touch. Pour the cooled filling into the crust. Refrigerate the pie for at least 4 hours or up to 24 hours.

6. Remove the tart from the refrigerator 20 minutes before serving, leaving it in the springform pan. Garnish with the coconut shavings and lemon zest. Remove the tart from the springform pan. To cut, grease your knife with a bit of coconut oil before slicing, adding more oil as needed between cuts.

Old-Fashioned Ice Cream Cake

WITH "OREO" COOKIE CRUMBLE

When we finally perfected this cake during one of our many hours of recipe testing, we started cheering, and Ashton, my wonderful recipe tester and all-around wizard, said, "I'm so happy that worked. You've been talking about this cake for over a year!" Let's backtrack. My eldest son has been obsessed with Oreo ice cream cake since he first tried it years ago at a friend's birthday party. He will happily accept the more natural alternatives to Oreos, and he devours coconut milk ice cream, but when it comes to Oreo ice cream cake he is more discerning. I set out to make his birthday dreams come true and came up with this cake. The almond and chocolate crumble tastes just like the chocolate cookie crumble you find on most conventional ice cream cakes, and the white chocolate drizzle takes this to the next level. You can make this with vegan or dairy ice cream. I've never found a cream-filled chocolate cookie without cane sugar, so if I'm just making this for a weekend dessert or pool party I stick to the recipe and everyone is thrilled, but on my son's birthday I buy the healthier chocolate sandwich cookies like Nature's Way or Newman's Own and break them up on top of the cake, much to his delight.

SERVES 8 TO 10

2 cups **almonds**

1 cup **dark chocolate chips**

2 tablespoons **pure maple syrup**

2 tablespoons plus ½ teaspoon **coconut oil**, melted

2 pints **nondairy chocolate ice cream**

2 pints **nondairy vanilla ice cream**

½ cup **white chocolate chips**

1. In a food processor, combine the almonds, chocolate chips, maple syrup, and 2 tablespoons of the coconut oil. Pulse until the nuts are finely ground and the mixture retains its shape when squeezed between your fingers. Press two-thirds of the crust mixture into an even layer over the bottom of a 9-inch springform pan. (Reserve the remaining crust mixture for topping.) Freeze the crust for 10 minutes. Remove the ice creams from the freezer to soften slightly.

2. Using a rubber spatula or offset spatula, spread the softened chocolate ice cream evenly over the bottom of the prepared crust. Freeze for 10 minutes, if needed, then repeat with the vanilla ice cream, spreading it into an even layer over the chocolate ice cream and smoothing the top. Top the cake with the reserved crust mixture.

3. Melt the white chocolate chips in a double boiler or in a heatproof bowl sitting over a pot of boiling water (make sure the bottom of the bowl doesn't touch the water). Drizzle the cake with the melted white chocolate and freeze for at least 6 hours or up to overnight.

4. Remove the cake from the freezer 10 minutes before serving to soften slightly. Release the springform pan and remove the ring to cut the cake.

Coconut and Carob Magic Cookie Bars

When I was young, my favorite Girl Scout cookies were Caramel deLites (formerly Samoas). My mom usually relented and would buy a box during Girl Scout season much to her chagrin. One day she showed up to school pickup with a mix between a magic bar and Caramel deLites. It was more a cluster than a bar, and she definitely never had a recipe, but to this day, I remember how delicious they were. My kids don't know what Samoas are, but they do know that they love these magic cookie bars. I always smile when I see them enjoying one, because it reminds me of elementary school and my excitement every time a box of Caramel deLites was passed around.

MAKES 16 BARS

8 tablespoons **coconut oil**, melted, plus more for greasing

1 cup **coconut flour**

1 cup **almond flour**

2 cups unsweetened **coconut flakes**

2 cups **carob chips**

3 tablespoons **date syrup**

¼ cup **sweetened condensed coconut milk**, homemade (recipe follows) or store-bought

1. Preheat the oven to 350°F. Grease an 8-inch-square or similar-size baking pan with coconut oil. Cut two pieces of parchment paper 3 to 4 inches larger than the prepared baking pan. Lay one of the parchment pieces across the pan, allowing the excess parchment to hang over the sides. Repeat with the second layer of parchment, perpendicular to the first.

2. In a food processor, combine the coconut flour, almond flour, and the melted coconut oil. Pulse briefly to combine, then continue to pulse or process until a dough forms, similar to the texture of damp sand; when squeezed between your fingers, it should hold together.

3. Press the crust mixture into an even layer over the bottom of the prepared pan. Bake the crust for 10 minutes, or until lightly browned and dry. Remove from the oven (keep the oven on) and allow the crust to cool completely, at least 15 minutes. (You can accelerate this process by placing the crust in the refrigerator for 10 to 15 minutes.)

4. In a medium bowl, mix together the coconut flakes and carob chips. Stir in the date syrup and sweetened condensed coconut milk until fully combined. Evenly spread this mixture on the cooled crust and return the pan to the oven. Bake for 12 to 15 minutes, until the coconut is lightly toasted and fragrant. Allow the cake to cool for at least 2 hours, then use the overhanging parchment to remove it from the pan and set it on a cutting board. Cut into squares and serve. Store in an airtight container for up to 5 days.

SWEETENED CONDENSED COCONUT MILK

MAKES ABOUT 1 CUP

1 (13.5-ounce) can full-fat coconut milk

¾ cup coconut sugar

In a small saucepan, bring the coconut milk and coconut sugar to a simmer over medium-low heat. Reduce the heat to low and simmer, stirring occasionally, until reduced by half, 20 to 25 minutes. Allow to cool completely before using, at least 30 minutes. The condensed coconut milk can be stored in an airtight container in the refrigerator for up to 2 weeks.

Classic Hot Chocolate

I've always been a hot chocolate lover, and my kids take after me. Maybe it's because we're a family of skiers and ice skaters, but hot chocolate is in high demand. To get the creaminess of classic hot chocolate, oat or soy milk works best here, but you can use any plant-based milk you prefer. I find that mixing cacao powder and chocolate really brings richness and decadence. I add better-for-you marshmallows such as Mojave Mallows or coconut whipped cream for fun.

SERVES 1

2 cups unsweetened **oat or soy milk**

2 tablespoons unsweetened **cacao powder**

1 tablespoon **dark chocolate chunks or chips**

1 to 2 tablespoons **date syrup**, to taste

Marshmallows or coconut whipped cream, for serving (optional)

In a small saucepan, heat the oat milk over medium heat until it just begins to bubble along the sides of the pan. Remove the pan from the heat and whisk in cacao powder and chocolate chips. Continue to whisk until the cacao and chocolate have fully melted and emulsified with the milk. Stir in the date syrup and serve hot, topped with marshmallows or coconut whipped cream, if desired.

"Instant" Hot Coconut Carob

Hot carob is a great alternative to hot chocolate if you want a caffeine-free hot drink that is also lower in sugar, as carob is naturally sweet and doesn't need added sugar. I make this almost daily in the winter, and the whole family enjoys it. It's indulgent but still feels healthy and nourishing. You can make it with any plant-based milk, but I love the extra creaminess of coconut milk, which makes this even more luxurious.

SERVES 1

1 tablespoon **carob powder**

1 tablespoon **carob chips**

Full-fat **coconut milk**, for serving

1. In a small saucepan, heat 2 cups of water over medium-high heat until the water begins to simmer. Remove the saucepan from the heat and whisk in the carob powder and carob chips. Continue to whisk until the carob has fully melted and emulsified with the water.

2. Pour the hot drink into a mug and finish with a desired amount of coconut milk. Serve hot.

Acknowledgments

I've wanted to write a book for as long as I can remember, and while the journey was not always clear or linear, I somehow knew that one day I would. I've been so fortunate to have a life filled with family and friends who have supported me, in ways big and small, as I took the time to follow my own path. Doing so is what allowed me to find my purpose, and this book to come to life.

To my parents: You have nourished and nurtured me my whole life; your love is immense. Thank you for having the knowledge and intuition to know that food is medicine. I am who I am because of you. Thank you for the gift of deep and unconditional love—without it, none of what I have accomplished would be possible, least of all this book.

To Michael, the best partner to be on this journey with. Thank you for always encouraging and uplifting me, especially during the crazy process of writing this book while also raising our three wild and beautiful boys. My number one taste tester, thanks for always saying "it's delicious!" Love you!

To Lukas, Dylan, and Oliver, my greatest teachers, my most fun and hilarious dinner dates, my favorite people to cook for, and my most creative and eager sous chefs—thank you for making me a mom, and for bringing me closer to myself.

To Ophelia and Bill: Words will never capture my gratitude for the love, encouragement, and joy that you have brought to my life, and for all you have done to support me in the pursuit of my dreams.

To Sammy, thank you for being my sister, too, and for the (pure) magic you bring to my life. And to David and Elle, thank you for always being so enthusiastic about my cooking.

To my grandmother Hazel, the ultimate hostess and chef: So much of me is because of you. I miss you so much, and I really hope you don't mind that I use cashew sour cream in your kugel recipe.

To my grandmother Ginny: I crave your lentil soup every day. Mom and I inherited our je ne sais quoi in the kitchen from you. I hold you in my heart.

To my aunt Beth: Not sure I would have made it through the teenage years—or, let's be real, any of the years—without you. A queen in the kitchen, a second mother, and the ultimate advice-giver.

To Beth Dewoody, for all the love, adventures, and support over the years.

To Alex and Scott, thank you for believing in this book from day one and for helping to make it a reality.

To Mara, I'll always marvel that we chose such similar paths. Thank you for being more of a sister than a cousin.

To Missy, the ultimate adventurer and trailblazer, thank you for inspiring me to explore the world and to move to Aspen after college to teach snowboarding; so much of my life unfolded when I took that chance. I hope you know that I have always looked up to you.

To Fiona, Eric, Sam, and Nick: You all mean so much to me—thank you for believing in me and in Spring Café Aspen. And yes, I'll always be *this* excited to see you, clapping excited.

To Kyle, my healthy-food soul-sister-cousin forever.

To Tatina, my tatsoi green.

To Carlton, for helping me bring Spring Café Aspen to life with your brilliant artwork and branding when I first had the idea. And to Sarah, for always being someone I can call, look up to, and cry and laugh with about motherhood, love, life, and all of it.

To Grant, for being my cheerleader and for taking every piece of health, grocery, and kitchenware advice that I've ever given you to heart—"I told you so." And to Madeleine, thank you for all the love and for believing in me when I wanted to open Spring Café Aspen in NYC.

Thank you to the indominable Sabrina Taitz. Without you, this book simply would not exist. You are tireless, fearless, bold, and absolutely brilliant, and most importantly, you believed so deeply in me that you made it impossible for everyone else not to. I'm not sure how I got so lucky to call you an agent, and a friend, but I am eternally grateful. And thank you for loving Spring Café Aspen as much as you love me.

To Claudia McPike, for remembering our conversation at the farmers' market, and my dream, and when the time was right, for making the call that would lead to this book.

To my editor, Caitlin Leffel: I guess it was destined from our first meeting at Spring all those years ago that we would work on this book together one day. Our story is a reminder that what is meant for you will always be yours, and to trust the divine timing of your life. The faith you put in me as a first-time author is a gift that I will always hold close to my heart. Thank you for your sharp edits and sage advice. To work with you is such a privilege, and I know how lucky I am.

To Amanda Englander, thank you for believing in me and taking a chance on me, and thank you for letting me tell this story in my own words. I still can't believe I got to work with you on this book; your brilliant and sharp eye took it to the next level.

To Renée Bollier, Lisa Forde, Kaylie Pendelton, and the entire Union Square & Co. team, thank you for all your time, energy, support, and enthusiasm. What a dream to make this book with all of you—I am the luckiest!

To Ashton Keefe: Who would have thought when we met on a photo shoot all those years ago that we would work on this book together! You knew, and you made me know it too. Thank you for turning my scribbles and "a pinch here and a carrot there" into legible recipes. We've had so much fun and made so many memories that I will cherish.

To Linda Pugliese: You brought this book to life with your photographs and your calm presence and generous spirit. I'm not sure anyone else could have captured the story I was hoping to tell. Thank you for all the time and care you gave to this project, and for making sure each shot was perfect. I'm so proud of this book and what we created together, and I hope to work with you again, and again.

To Monica Pierini, food stylist extraordinaire, thank you for making it all look so beautiful, for teaching me tricks of the trade, and mostly for being an absolute joy to work with. I will never forget all the laughs, your gorgeous food, or your birthday carob ganache.

To Megan Litt, my fellow Aries Swiftie, thanks for all the joy you brought to set, for understanding my millennial ways, and for imbuing my food with your delightful touch.

To Paige Hicks, you told this story so perfectly with your whimsical and stunning prop styling—family, food, fun, love, laughter, and joy. And my kitchen cabinets are overflowing because of you. I adore you!

To Eva, Ally, and Halle, thank you for working so hard alongside me to make sure this book was a success, and for always saying yes every time I say I have a dream or an idea for what's next.

To Laura Vogel, thank you for coming into my life, understanding my vision, and helping me take the next steps.

To Corinna, I think I'd be lost without you. You understand me perfectly and the story I'm trying to tell. Thank you for working with my wild schedule, for the endless pep talks, and for encouraging me to be more of me, every time I feel uncertain.

To Blanca Salas, without you, there would be no Spring Café Aspen. Thank you for answering my call all those years ago and for a decade of delicious food made with love, care, and magic. And for Karla, Chula, and Layton, always.

To my team at Spring Café Aspen: There's no way I could run restaurants without all of you. Thank you from the bottom of my heart.

To Adam Rand, for your advice between wisdom, brilliance, and, above all, loyalty and friendship. Thank you.

To Jessie, for being my sister in this life. I am the luckiest.

To Moni, for almost twenty years of the truest kind of friendship, and for taking my hand and being the voice of reason whenever I feel lost.

To Taryn, my favorite person to cook, co-mom, shop, and dream with: Thank you for reminding me I am the light whenever I forget. You are, too.

To Lily: You are sunshine, warmth, and kindness personified. And to Doug, thank you for always answering my call. You both are the definition of friends who are family.

To Jenn: You came into my life when I needed it most and our paths crossed exactly as they were meant to. I wouldn't have made it through the chaos and wonder of these past few years without you. My surf sister and my confidante, I can't wait to see all the places and waves life takes us. I know that we'll be surfing, cooking, and adventuring forever. Thank you for being there for me the way that you have.

To Melissa, there are no words to thank you for all the ways you have supported me and Spring, but it's the quiet moments over green juice and matcha, full of laughter and tears, that I hold closest to my heart.

To Daphne, for holding my hand during every step of the process of writing this book, and for being the kind of friend who shines their considerable light on others.

To Danielle Duboise, for making Spring your second kitchen, and for your shining sisterhood and support.

To Mollie, for always listening and loving.

To Nicole Fasolino, for the hours spent on the phone and on the floor of my closet—you are the bravest person I know, and the embodiment of love.

To Arielle, for being a wonderful friend and for taking my phone all those years ago, creating @springbysabrina with me, and telling me it was time to share my knowledge and story with a bigger audience. Without you and that moment, this book might not exist.

To Alana, thank you for showing up for me and for being my Aries partner in crime—you always understand me.

To Stef, for so many years of love and loyalty.

To my school moms turned lifers, Caroline, Tracey, Chelsa, Meg, and Lindz. I'm forever grateful our kids brought us together.

To Alexa: We are still young and full of hope, you have carried my heart so many times, and your beautiful sweaters brought these pages to life.

To Tiare: Landing on you was the best meet cute, and now we can surf and be sisters forever.

Thank you for teaching me how to edit this book in Adobe!

To Rebecca Rittenhouse: My beautiful friend, some people come in and stay, thank goodness you are one of them.

To Anastasia, I don't like to think about what life would be like if I'd never sat next to you at lunch all those years ago. Thank you for letting me talk about the same thing as many times as I need to, and for always knowing when I need a hug and a kugel sister.

To Liz, the most special soul I know. I love you—thank you for showing me what following your heart and intuition truly means.

To Britt: Would we have survived early motherhood without each other? I'm not sure I know the answer to that question, and I'm glad I never have to find out. No one understands it all the way you do—so happy we have each other on this journey.

To Gloria: You inspire me in the kitchen and in life, you do it all with ease and grace and, above all, kindness.

To Tracy Anderson, for over a decade of friendship, for telling me to run toward my dreams, and for teaching me to move in a way that fills my soul with joy.

To Amy Griffin, I have endless gratitude for the blessings you've brought to my life. Thank you for believing in me and investing in me. Thank you for telling me when it was okay to not be okay, and for being such a guiding light and force in my life.

To Mariel: You should be here, but I always feel your presence. I know you would have loved this book and the journey that led to writing it, and I also know you've been with me every step of the way, gently encouraging me.

To my brothers from others sisters, Pete, Scotty, Daniel Low, Sam Blank and Nicks, thanks for always having my back. On land and in the water.

To Matt, for spending twenty-one straight days in the water with me and changing the course of my life, and for always reminding me that it's okay to be scared but to do it anyway.

To Olivier, for your magic and healing touch all these years.

To Patty and Dr. Ofgang: Not many people can say they have had the same doctor since they were two years old. Your knowledge and care are unparalleled.

To Mark, for the utmost care, brilliance, and compassion.

To David: Your guidance is immeasurable.

To Stephen, for your wisdom.

To Lindsay Greene Tulchin, for setting me on the path to true healing, for seeing me in my darkest hour, and for helping me see myself too.

To my high school teachers Chris Goulian, Lisa Berrol, Matt Ives, and Ron Rothenberg, for instilling in me a love of learning and a deep curiosity that has continued to guide and inspire me throughout my life.

To my college professors Chis Kluge, Ana Sun, and Crystal Parikh, you showed me that the pursuit of knowledge is a lifelong journey, and you encouraged me to think, grow and explore in my own way. The lessons I learned in your seminars, still echo throughout my life and work.

For James McBride, your class made me the writer I always hoped I could be and helped me find my voice. I still pull out yellow legal pads whenever I really want to get something down on paper. You told me to keep writing and one day I'd be published, and you were right. What a profound blessing to be your student. Thank you.

For Eden, thank you for working by my side, for keeping me sane and organized, and for always knowing what to do when I don't.

To Jessica Kisling: You know you're my boy-mom icon. I don't know how you do all that you do, but it inspires me every day, as does everything you cook. Thank you for always being there for me.

To Pok, Gaga, Joss, and Ula, there's literally no chance I could do any of this without all of you. Thank you for all the love, joy, and care you bring to my life. Thank you for cooking with me and inspiring me, and for putting up with all my mess and chaos while I tested, retested, and filmed these recipes and experimented in the science lab that is our kitchen.

And finally, to all of you, my readers, diners, and Instagram followers who have made this dream career, and this book, possible. Thank you for letting me show up every day as my whole self, for trusting me, engaging with me, buying this book, and supporting me. I have no words but to say thank you, thank you, thank you from the bottom of my heart.

Index

NOTE: Page references in *italics* refer to photos of recipes.

D

E

F

G

H

I

J

K

L

M

N

O

P